CAMBRIDGE ECONOMIC HANDBOOKS.—1
GENERAL EDITOR: C. W. GUILLEBAUD, M. A.

SUPPLY AND DEMAND

SUPPLY AND DEMAND

BY

HUBERT D. HENDERSON

M.A.

.FELLOW OF ALL SOULS COLLEGE, OXFORD ;
FORMERLY FELLOW OF CLARE COLLEGE, CAMBRIDGE

London

NISBET & CO. LTD.

Cambridge

AT THE UNIVERSITY PRESS

First published December *1921*
Reprinted   November *1924*
  ,,   *October*   *1926*
  ,,   *March*   *1928*
  ,,   *July*   *1930*
Revised edition May   *1932*
Reprinted   January *1936*
  ,,   *March*   *1938*
  ,,   *October*   *1940*
  ,,   *November*   *1941*
  ,,   *April*   *1943*
  ,,   *January*   *1945*
  ,,   *December*   *1945*
  ,,   *January*   *1946*
  ,,   *February*   *1947*
  ,,   *September* *1947*

INTRODUCTION TO THE SERIES

By the General Editor

SHORTLY after the war of 1914–18 there seemed to be a place for a Series of introductory Economic Handbooks " intended to convey to the ordinary reader and to the uninitiated student some conception of the general principles of thought which economists now apply to economic problems ".

This Series was planned by the late Lord Keynes under the title *Cambridge Economic Handbooks*, and he wrote for it a general Editorial Introduction of which the words quoted above formed part. In 1936 Lord Keynes handed over the editorship of the Series to Mr. D. H. Robertson, who held it until he became Professor of Economics in the University of London.[1]

The judgment of its originators has been justified by the wide welcome given to the Series. Apart from its circulation in the British Empire, it has been published from the start in the United States of America while translations of the principal volumes have so far appeared in German, Spanish, Italian, Swedish, Japanese, Polish and Lithuanian.

It is symptomatic of the changes which have been taking place in recent times in the development of economic science, changes associated in a high degree with the work and influence of Lord Keynes himself, that within the brief space of fifteen years the text of part of the Editorial Introduction should have stood in need of revision. In its original version the last paragraph of the Introduction to the Series ran as follows :

---

[1] Professor Robertson now holds the Chair of Political Economy in the University of Cambridge.

" Even on matters of principle there is not yet a complete unanimity of opinion amongst professors. Generally speaking, the writers of these volumes believe themselves to be orthodox members of the Cambridge School of Economics. At any rate, most of their ideas about the subject, and even their prejudices, are traceable to the contact they have enjoyed with the writings and lectures of the two economists who have chiefly influenced Cambridge thought for the past fifty years, Dr. Marshall and Professor Pigou."

When the Editorship of the Series was transferred to Mr. D. H. Robertson, Lord Keynes consented to the retention of his general Introduction, but subsequently re-wrote the concluding paragraph in the following form :

" Even on matters of principle there is not yet a complete unanimity of opinion amongst professional students of the subject. Immediately after the war daily economic events were of such a startling character as to divert attention from theoretical complexities. But to-day, economic science has recovered its wind. Traditional treatments and traditional solutions are being questioned, improved, and revised. In the end this activity of research should clear up controversy. But for the moment controversy and doubt are increased. The writers of this series must apologize to the general reader and to the beginner if many parts of their subject have not yet reached to a degree of certainty and lucidity which would make them easy and straightforward reading."

Still more recent events have produced a world so far removed from that which existed when the foregoing words were written, that it has fallen to the lot of the present Editor to provide a new Introduction.

This is perhaps a good vantage point from which to survey very briefly some of the principal trends in the evolution of economic thought in this country during the past thirty years.   Prior to 1914 economic theory here was largely dominated by Alfred Marshall ; and economists, following him, thought in terms of the long period tendencies of the different sections of the economic system towards positions of equilibrium, even though ever-present dynamic factors were perpetually modifying the existing structure and presenting new and equally distant, if equally unattainable, goals as stimuli to change and adaptation.   Moreover, in the Marshallian system, those tendencies resulted from the working of persistent underlying forces which were conceived of as largely competitive in character.   The increasing trend towards monopoly was certainly affecting thought, but not so much in the realm of the theory of value, as in the emphasis which came to be laid on possible discrepancies between the private interest and the social interest. Under the influence of Professor Pigou a Welfare Economics was developing side by side with, and out of, the Value Economics of the older generation.

After 1918 the long-drawn-out agony of the depressed areas, the weakening of the position of this country in international trade, and the tremendous intensity of the economic crisis of 1930–32 (to mention but a few out of the many contributing causes) combined, on the one hand, to focus attention on problems of the short period and, on the other hand, to throw doubt on the extent to which the self-adjusting, seemingly automatic mechanism, which on the whole had operated so effectively during the nineteenth century, was capable of coping with the deep-seated maladjustments and disharmonies which characterized the post-war world. At the same time value theory itself was profoundly influenced by the emergence of a number of writers who approached value problems from the view-point of monopoly, and emphasized the unrealistic nature of an analysis which was based on the assumptions of perfect competition and a perfect market. Most of all, however, economic thought was dominated by the desire to find a solution for the problem of how to maintain the level of effective demand so as to avoid the recurrence of phases of deep depression and widespread unemployment. There was a growing feeling of impatience with the economics of the long period " in which we are all dead," and a great perhaps even excessive, concentration on the short period in which we live and move and have our being.

The result was a remarkable ferment of ideas, the challenging of ancient orthodoxies, and " for the moment controversy and doubt [were] increased ". This ferment had by no means subsided when the second war with Germany broke out in September 1939, bringing in its train a degree of State interference with the normal peace-time working of the economic system far exceeding that reached even in the last years of the war of 1914–18.

In so far as it is possible to foresee future trends, they would seem to lie in a much greater measure of conscious public control over many aspects of economic activity than has existed in the past. It will no doubt still remain true, to quote Lord Keynes's Introduction again, that :

" The Theory of Economics does not furnish a body of settled conclusions immediately applicable to policy. It is a method rather than a doctrine, an apparatus of the mind, a technique of thinking, which helps its possessor to draw correct conclusions."

Nevertheless, economists may well find themselves to a greater degree than hitherto called upon to express their views on matters of economic policy, and—for a time at least—the writers of future volumes of the Cambridge Economic Handbooks may be concerned rather with specific problems than with the more general aspects of economic theory.

C. W. G.

Cambridge,
  JULY, 1946.

CONTENTS

CHAPTER I

THE ECONOMIC WORLD

CHAPTER II

THE GENERAL LAWS OF SUPPLY AND DEMAND

CHAPTER III

UTILITY AND THE MARGIN OF CONSUMPTION

CHAPTER IV

COST AND THE MARGIN OF PRODUCTION

CHAPTER V

JOINT DEMAND AND SUPPLY

CONTENTS

CHAPTER VI

LAND

CHAPTER VII

RISK-BEARING AND ENTERPRISE

CHAPTER VIII

CAPITAL

CHAPTER IX

LABOUR

CHAPTER X

THE REAL COSTS OF PRODUCTION

SUPPLY AND DEMAND

CHAPTER I

THE ECONOMIC WORLD

§ 1. *Theory and Fact.* The controversy between the
" Theorist " and the " Practical Man " is common to
all branches of human affairs, but it is more than usually
prevalent, and perhaps more than usually acrid in the
economic sphere. It is always a rather foolish controversy, and I have no intention of entering into it, but
its prevalence makes it desirable to emphasize a plati-
tude. Economic theory must be based upon actual
fact : indeed, it must be essentially an attempt, like all
theory, to *describe* the actual facts in proper sequence,
and in true perspective ; and if it does not do this it is
an imposture. Moreover, the facts which economic
theory seeks to describe are primarily economic facts,
facts, that is to say, which emerge in, and are concerned
with, the ordinary business world ; and it is, therefore,
mainly upon such facts that the theory must be based.
People sometimes speak as though they supposed the
economist to start from a few psychological assumptions
(e.g. that a man is actuated mainly by his own self-
interest) and to build up his theories upon such founda-

tions by a process of pure reasoning. When, therefore, some advance in the study of psychology throws into apparent disrepute such ancient maxims about human nature, these people are disposed to conclude that the old economic theory is exploded, since its psychological premises have been shown to be untrue. Such an attitude involves a complete misunderstanding not merely of economics, but of the processes of human thought. It is quite true that the various branches of knowledge are interrelated very intimately, and that an advance in one will often suggest a development in another. By all means let the economist and psychologist avoid a pedantic specialism and let each stray into the other's province whenever he thinks fit. But the fact remains that they are primarily concerned with different things : and that each is most to be trusted when he is upon his own ground. When, therefore, the economist indulges in a generalization about psychology, even when he gives it as a reason for an economic proposition, in nine cases out of ten the economics will not depend upon the psychology ; the psychology will rather be an inference (and very possibly a crude and hasty one) from the economic facts of which he is tolerably sure.

But the purpose of economic theory is not merely to describe the facts of the economic world ; it is to describe them in their proper sequence and true perspective. It must begin with those facts which are most general and which have the widest possible significance. Those are not likely to be the facts which our practical experience forces most insistently upon our notice. For it is the particular and not the general, the differences between things rather than their resemblances, that concern us most in daily life. Nor are we likely to find the universal facts which we require in the sphere of public controversy. We must rather look for them in the dark recesses of our consciousness, where are stored those truths which are so obvious that we hardly notice them, which are so indisputable that we seldom examine them, which seem so trite that we are apt to miss their full significance.

§ 2. *The Division of Labour.* There is one such truth in the economic sphere which it is essential to appreciate vividly and fully, with the widest sweep of the imagination and the sharpest clarity of thought. Man lives by co-operating with his fellow-men. In the modern world, that co-operation is of a boundless range and an indescribable complexity. Yet it is essentially undesigned and uncontrolled by man. The humblest inhabitant of Great Britain or the United States depends for the satisfaction of his simplest needs upon the activities of innumerable people, in every walk of life and in every corner of the globe. The ordinary commodities which appear upon his dinner table represent the final product of the labours of a medley of merchants, farmers, seamen, engineers, workers of almost every craft. But there is no human authority presiding over this great complex of labour, organizing the various units, and directing them towards the common ends which they subserve. Wheel upon wheel, in a ceaseless succession of interdependent processes, the business world revolves : but no one has planned and no one guides the intricate mechanism whose smooth working is so vital to us all.

B

Man, indeed, can organize and has organized much. Within a large factory the efforts of thousands of work-people, each engaged on the repetition of a single small process, are fitted together so as to form an ordered whole by the conscious direction of the management. Sometimes factory is joined with factory, with farms, fisheries, mines, with transport and distributing agencies, as one gigantic business unit, controlled by a common will. These giant businesses are remarkable achievements of man's organizing gifts. The individuals who control them wield an immense power, which so impresses the public imagination that we dub them " kings," " supermen," " Napoleons of industry." But, how small a portion of man's economic life is dominated by such men! Even as regards the affairs of their own businesses, how narrow, after all, are the limits of their influence! The prices at which they can buy their materials and borrow their capital, the quantities of their products which the public will consume, are factors at once vital to their prosperity and outside their own control.

A great business, like a nation, may cherish visions of self-sufficiency, may stretch its tentacles forward to the consumer and backwards to its supplies of raw material ; but each fresh extension of its activities serves only to multiply its points of contact with the outside world. When those points are reached, the largest business, like the smallest, is out on the open sea of an economic system immeasurably larger and more powerful than itself. There it must meet—the better perhaps for its inherent strength and accumulated knowledge—the impact of rude forces, which it is powerless to control.

Beneath the blasts of a trade depression, or some other tendency of world-wide scope, the authority of the mightiest industrial magnate, and equally of any Government, assumes the same essential insignificance as the pride of a man humbled by contact with the elemental powers of nature.

§ 3. *The Existence of Order.* The parallel can be pursued further with advantage. Just as in the world of natural phenomena, which for long seemed to man so wayward and inexplicable, we have come gradually to perceive an all-pervading uniformity and order ; so there is manifest in the economic world, uniformity, order, of a similar if less majestic kind. Upon the co-operation of his fellowmen, man depends for the very means of life : yet he takes this co-operation for granted, with a complacent confidence and often with a naïve unconsciousness, as he takes the rising of to-morrow's sun. The reliability of this unorganized co-operation has powerfully impressed the imagination of many observers.

" On entering Paris which I had come to visit," exclaimed Bastiat in the mid-nineteenth century, " I said to myself—Here are a million of human beings who would all die in a short time if provisions of every kind ceased to flow towards this great metropolis. Imagination is baffled when it tries to appreciate the vast multiplicity of commodities which must enter to-morrow through the barriers in order to preserve the inhabitants from falling a prey to the convulsions of famine, rebellion, and pillage. And yet all sleep at this moment, and their peaceful slumbers are not disturbed for a single instant by the prospect of such a frightful catastrophe. On the other hand, eighty departments have been labouring to-day, without concert, without any mutual understanding, for the provisioning of Paris."

The theme may well excite wonder. But wonder should always be watched with a wary eye ; for he is apt to bring in his train a hanger-on called worship, who can do nothing but mischief here. It is a short step from a passage like that quoted above to a glorification of the existing system of society, to a defence of all manner of indefensible things, and a cross-grained attitude towards all projects of reform. It is a short step ; but it is one which it is quite unjustifiable to take. For the evils of our economic system are too plain to be ignored ; too many people have harsh personal experience of the wastefulness of its production, the injustice of its distribution ; of its sweating, its unemployment and slums. And when the attempt is made to plaster over evils such as these with obsequious rhetoric about the majesty of economic law, it is not surprising that the spirit of many men should revolt and that they should retort by denying the existence of order in the business world, by declaring that the spectacle which *they* see is one of discord, confusion and chaos. And then we are engulfed in a controversy as stale, flat and unprofitable as that between the " theorist " and the " practical man."

The truth is that the language of praise and obloquy is quite inappropriate. In the first place, it may be well to note that the order of which I have spoken manifests itself not merely in those economic phenomena which are beneficial to man, but hardly less in those which work to his hurt. Even in those alternations of good and bad trade, which spell so much unemployment and misery, there is discernible a rhythmic regularity like that of the process of the seasons, or the ebb and flow of the tide. This is not an elegance to be admired. Furthermore, in so far as the order comprises adjustments and tendencies which are beneficial (as, indeed, is mainly true), there is no warrant for assuming that these are either adequate to secure a prosperous community or dependent upon the social arrangements which happen to exist. Let us, therefore, refrain from premature polemics and examine in a spirit of detachment some further aspects of the elaborate, but yet unorganized, co-operation of which so much has been already said.

§ 4. *Some Reflections upon Joint Products.* A quite inadequate idea of the complexity of this co-operation is obtained by dwelling on the numbers of people who participate in it, or the immense distances over which it extends. The deficiency can be partially supplied by referring to some of the more obvious of the many subtle interconnections which exist between different commodities and different trades.

There are innumerable groups of commodities (which it is customary to term " joint products ") such that the production of one commodity belonging to the group necessarily implies or very greatly facilitates the production of the others. Wool and mutton ; beef and hides ; cotton and cotton-seed are a few familiar illustrations. The important feature of these " joint products " is the fairly precise relation which must exist between the quantities in which the different products are supplied. If you plant a certain crop of cotton, it will yield you so much cotton lint (i.e. raw cotton) and so much cotton-seed. You can, of course, if you choose, throw away part of the seed, as indeed at one time planters used to do; but unless you do this, you cannot vary the proportions of the two things which you will have for sale. Similarly, if you keep a flock of sheep, or a herd of cattle, you will obtain wool and mutton in the one case, or beef and hides in the other, in proportions, which indeed you can vary within certain limits by choosing a different breed,[1] but which you cannot radically transform. When, however, we turn to the uses to which these products are put, no similar relation is to be discovered. Cotton lint is used chiefly for making articles of clothing; cotton-seed for crushing into oil, on the one hand, and cake for cattle fodder on the other. There is no apparent connection of any kind between the demands for these different things, and still less is there any obvious reason why these demands should bear to one another the particular proportions which characterize their respective supplies. It is very much the same with wool and mutton; with beef and hides; with all "joint products." Why should we consume mutton on the one hand and woollen clothing on the other, in a ratio at all commensurate with that in which they are yielded by the sheep?

What, then, might we expect to find if order was non-existent in the economic world? Surely that some things such as wool would be produced in quantities

---

[1] These possibilities of small variation are of very great importance as will be shown in Chapter V, but they do not affect the present argument.

many times in excess of the demand for them, quite possibly five, ten, or twenty times in excess; while conversely the supplies of others such as mutton might fall far short of what was required. But in practice we find nothing of the sort. Somehow it comes about that an equilibrium is established between the demand for and the supply of every commodity; and that this applies to wool and mutton, to beef and hides, as surely as to commodities which are produced quite independently. It is true that this equilibrium is a rough, imperfect one; and it may happen that what is called a " glut " of wool may co-exist for a short period with what is called a scarcity of mutton. But qualifications of this nature are in the strictest sense of the phrase, the exceptions which prove the rule. For the departures from equilibrium which gluts and scarcities represent are always transient and are usually confined within narrow limits. A strong prevailing trend towards an adjustment of demand and supply is unmistakably manifest amid all the vagaries of changing circumstance.

Let me carry the argument a step further for the benefit of any reader who is restrained by a repugnance too deep and instinctive to be readily overcome, from admitting fairly to his mind that conception of order which I am endeavouring to emphasize. He will in all probability be one who, cherishing ideals of a better and fairer system of society, looks forward to a time when an organized co-operation will be substituted for what he regards as the existing chaos. Let us suppose that his visions were fulfilled as completely as he could desire; and that an immense system of Socialism were in existence, embracing not one country only, but the whole world. Suppose all the difficulties of human perversity and administrative technique to have been surmounted and a wise, disinterested executive to be in supreme control of our business life. Let us suppose all this, and ask only the question : How would this executive treat the humdrum case of wool and mutton ? How would it decide the number of sheep it would maintain ?

Shall we suppose that it is inspired by the ideal " to each according to his need," and that it resolves accordingly that the commodities which people require for a decent standard of life shall be supplied to them as a matter of course ? How, then, would it proceed ? It might estimate the amount of woollen clothing which a normal family requires, allowing for differences in climate, and possibly indulging somewhat the caprices of human taste. On this basis, a certain number of sheep would be indicated. It might perform a similar calculation for mutton, and again a certain number of sheep would be indicated. But it would be an extraordinary coincidence if the numbers which resulted from these independent calculations were nearly equal to one another, or were even of the same order of magnitude ; and, if they differed widely, what number would our world executive select ? Would it decide to waste an immense quantity of either wool or mutton ; or would it decide that it could not, after all, supply the full human needs for one or other of the commodities ?

Of course, if the executive were sensible it could solve the problem satisfactorily enough. It could retain the monetary system we know to-day and it could supply the commodities to the consumers, not as a matter of

right, but by selling them to them *at a price*. This price
it could then move upwards or downwards, raising, say,
the price of mutton and reducing that of wool, until it
found that the consumption of the two things was
adjusted in the required ratio. But if it acted in this
manner, what essentially would it be doing ? It would
be seeking by deliberate contrivance to reproduce, in
respect of this particular problem, the very conditions
which occur to-day without aim or effort on the part of
anyone at all.

The moral of this illustration must not be misin-
terpreted. It does not show the folly of Socialism or the
superiority of Laissez-faire. What it does show is the
existence in the economic world of an order more
profound and more permanent than any of our social
schemes, and equally applicable to them all.

§ 5. *Some Reflections upon Capital*. Another aspect
of the great co-operation is of even greater significance.
It embraces not only a multitude of living men, but it
links the present together with the future and the past.
The goods and services which we enjoy to-day we owe
only in part to the labours of the week, the month, or
the year, only in part even to the efforts of our contem-
poraries. The men, long since dead and forgotten, who
built our railways, or sunk our coal mines, or engaged
in any of a great variety of tasks, are still contributing
to the satisfaction of our daily wants. The expression
is not altogether fanciful ; for, had it not been reasonable
to expect that those labours would be of use to us to-day,
many of them in all probability would never have been
undertaken. It was to meet our present wants, and

even our future wants, that many men toiled on monotonous tasks ten, twenty, thirty years ago. And yet, of course, we should deceive ourselves if we supposed that this was the motive of these men, that our welfare was the centre of their heart's desire. We in our turn dedicate to the future, and often to a distant future, an immense portion of our energies. Let any reader who doubts this, study the statistics of the occupations of the people, and reflect on how long a period must elapse before the labours of this trade or that can fulfil their ultimate function. How long would the period be in the case of a man making bricks, which will later be employed in the erection of a factory, where machinery will be made, to equip an electrical generating station designed to supply, over a period of many years, light, heat, and power to people living in a remote Continent ? A longer time, it may be hazarded, than he is accustomed to look ahead.

Like the daily co-operation of living men, this co-operation of past, present and future is essential to the well-being of mankind, and yet it is undesigned and unorganized. As private individuals, men do, indeed, deliberately provide for their own future, and for that of their kith and kin : as the directors of businesses, they try to forecast the trend of demand. But such conscious calculations and deliberate acts would avail little if they stood alone. They are hardly more than the necessary spokes in the great wheel which regulates the relations of past, present and future. The hub of the wheel is an elaborate system of borrowing and lending, essentially similar to the buying and selling of commodities. The private individual in order to provide

for his family or for his old age " saves " and " invests."
But what exactly does this mean ? It means that he
transfers so much purchasing power, which he might
have spent on his personal pleasures, to some one else
in return for the expectation of receiving, year by year
in the future, he and his heirs after him, a certain smaller
quantity of purchasing power. The other party to the
transaction will be, we may suppose, a business man who
enters into it because he sees the opportunity of a
promising industrial development, to undertake which he
requires more purchasing power than he himself possesses.
And, because this transaction is entered into, a smaller
number of us will shortly be engaged in making motor-
cars, or gramophones, and a larger number of us in
making factories and machinery, which will later
enhance the world's productive power.

Many transactions of the kind take place daily in
modern communities, and their multiplicity gives rise
to a mass of phenomena with which we are all tolerably
familiar. We recognize a short-loan market, a stock
exchange, a number of " markets " where lenders and
borrowers are brought together by the aid of various
intermediaries, such as banks, bill brokers, and stock
jobbers, who correspond to dealers in commodities.
Between these different specialized markets, we are aware
of an interconnection so close and strong that we speak
more generally of a Capital Market, of which the stock
exchange, the short-loan market and so forth, are the
component parts. Now, " market " is a word which was
originally used to denote a place where tangible commodities were bought and sold ; and the more closely
we examine the phenomena of the Capital Market, the

more closely do we perceive the profound resemblance between the mechanism of borrowing and lending, and that of buying and selling. Corresponding to the price of a commodity is the rate of interest (in the short-loan market we actually call the rate of discount " the price of money," and speak of money being cheap or dear) ; and between the rate of interest, the demand for and the supply of capital there exist relations precisely similar to those between price, demand, and supply in commodity markets. Above all there is the same strong prevailing trend towards an adjustment of demand and supply.

This fundamental resemblance between two such apparently incommensurable things as the buying of material commodities and the borrowing of capital is highly significant ; it is another instance of that order in the economic world, of which the reader may now be growing weary. But so difficult is it to see clearly and fully something which one sees, as it were, every day of one's life, that a few more moments of reflection on the special case of capital will be time well spent. Let us revert then to our fantasy of a world socialist commonwealth ; and humbly submit another poser to its supreme executive. The question this time will be whether some great constructional work, such, let us say, as the much discussed Severn barrage scheme, should or should not be undertaken. Let us suppose that the costs and future benefits of the undertaking can be estimated accurately ; and that the problem reduces itself to one of expending now a sum, let us say, of £20,000,000, with the prospects of obtaining in the future an income of power, or whatever it may be, worth

£1,000,000 per annum. I have assumed for the sake of simplicity that we shall still be reckoning in terms of money, though possibly the executive may have substituted Marxian labour units; but it is quite immaterial to the present argument what the measuring rod may be. The point to be observed is, that it is impossible to tackle the problem at all without the conception of a rate of interest. For suppose that you tried to do without it, and said, " We shall take a long view. The interests of the future are no less our concern than those of the present; we shall not discriminate between them. We shall regard as an enterprise worthy to be undertaken whatever promises to yield in the course of time a return larger than the outlay." Where will this lead you? The particular proposal set out above would clearly pass the test; for in twenty years the resultant benefits would have added up to a figure equivalent to the initial cost. But equally clearly, the cost might have been more than £20,000,000; it might have been £50,000,000, £100,000,000, whatever figure you care to take, and if you extend the period similarly to fifty or one hundred years, sooner or later the gains would top the cost. Now there is no limit to the enterprises which would pay their way on this basis; and it would be quite impossible to undertake them all. For they would swallow up all and more than all your labour and your materials, and would leave you with no resources with which to meet the recurrent daily wants of men. Clearly, then, in some way or other, you must pick and choose, you must reject some enterprizes as *insufficiently* worth while. But how would you proceed to choose? Without a clear principle, a simple criterion to guide you, you would be plunged in utter chaos. You could not say, "Let all proposals involving capital expenditure be submitted to a central committee, who shall compare them with one another in a sort of competitive examination and, after deciding the number of applications they can pass on the basis of the volume of resources which they can devote to the future, award the places to those which head the list." Such a prospect is a nightmare of officialism and delay. You would be driven to formulate a simple, intelligible rule or measure, and leave that rule to be applied by the unfettered judgment of innumerable men to individual problems, as and when they arose. And for such a rule or measure, you could not do better than a rate of interest; you would have to lay it down that only those projects should be approved which seemed likely to yield a return of 6 per cent, or whatever it might be. Even in deciding what it should be, the limits of your choice would be narrowly confined. If, for instance, you fixed on 1 or 2 per cent, you would probably discover that you had not achieved your object, that the undertakings for distant returns which passed this test, still consumed far more resources than you could spare. You would be compelled then to raise the rate until it had cut these enterprises down within manageable limits. But, once more, what essentially would you be doing? You would be using the instrument of the rate of interest to adjust the demand for and supply of capital, though indeed the interest might not be paid away as now to private individuals. You would be reproducing by the method of deliberate trial and error, the adjustments which occur automatically as things are, in the actual world. Once again the most perfectly contrived Utopia would be compelled to pay to the unorganized co-operation of our epoch the sincerest flattery of imitation.

§ 6. *The Fundamental Character of many Economic Laws.* But again perhaps a word of warning may be desirable. There is much controversy in these days about something called "Capitalism" or "The capitalist system." When these words are used with any precision, they usually refer to the arrangement so prevalent at present, whereby the ownership and sole ultimate control of a business rests with those who hold its stocks and shares. There is much to be said upon the merits and demerits of this system; but I shall not discuss it here. Nothing that I have said so far has any real bearing on it whatsoever; to suppose that it has, is indeed to miss the whole point of this chapter.

The order, which I have sought to reveal, pervading and moving the most diverse phenomena of the economic world, would be a far less noteworthy and impressive thing were it merely the peculiar product of capitalism. Merchant adventurers, companies, and trusts; Guilds, Governments and Soviets may come and go. But under them all, and, if need be, in spite of them all, the profound adjustments of supply and demand will work themselves out and work themselves out again for so long as the lot of man is darkened by the curse of Adam.

CHAPTER II

THE GENERAL LAWS OF SUPPLY AND DEMAND

§ 1. *Preliminary Statement of Three Laws.* The recognition of order in any branch of natural phenomena is but the prelude to the formulation of a set of laws, the simpler as the order is more universal, which describe, and as we say, explain it. Thus the perception of the even, elliptical courses of the heavenly bodies led to the statement of the law of gravitation and the laws of motion.

In economics, similar laws have long since been enunciated, and have proved themselves such valuable instruments for the understanding of the daily problems of the workaday world, that they have been woven into the texture of our ordinary speech and thought. I have already touched upon them in the preceding chapter. But it is now desirable to set them out in order, in the most concise and formal manner possible.

I. When, at the price ruling, demand exceeds supply, the price tends to rise. Conversely when supply exceeds demand the price tends to fall.

II. A rise in price tends, sooner or later, to decrease demand and to increase supply. Conversely a fall in price tends, sooner or later, to increase demand and to decrease supply.

III. Price tends to the level at which demand is equal to supply.

These three laws are the cornerstone of economic theory. They are the framework into which all analysis of special, detailed problems must be fitted. Their scope is very wide. I have purposely refrained from introducing into my statement of them any reference to commodities; for they extend far beyond commodities. Subject to an important qualification, they apply to capital, the price paid for the use of capital being what we call the rate of interest. They apply hardly less to " services," to the remuneration of labour of every kind and grade. People sometimes protest warmly against the idea of treating labour " like a commodity." If this indignation expresses no more than a belief that in matters concerning conditions of work, and relations between employees and the management, the sensibilities of human nature should be taken into due account, it is based on elementary decency and commonsense. But if, as sometimes appears, it is directed against the fact that the renumeration of labour is controlled by the laws of supply and demand, it is a mere baying at the moon, with singularly little provocation. For these laws are in no way peculiar to commodities, and it is no one's fault that they include commodities too within their scope.

But let us go back to the laws themselves. and probe

C

them and dissect them, and turn them this way and that, so that we may perceive their full content, and grasp it firmly in our minds. The third law implies a prevailing tendency for demand to be equal to supply. This tendency, as was suggested in Chapter I, can be verified by anyone from his experience and observation (provided he is a reasonable person, and not the tiresome kind who would dispute the law of gravitation because he sees that a feather falls to the ground more slowly than a stone). But it can also be deduced as a corollary from the two preceding laws ; and to regard it in this way will help us to appreciate its significance. Start, for instance, by supposing that demand is in excess of supply. Then the price will tend to rise. After the price has risen, the supply will become larger, while the demand will fall away. The excess of demand with which we started will thus clearly be diminished. But if there remains any portion of this excess, the same reactions will continue ; the price will rise further, and for the same reason ; demand will be further checked and supply further stimulated. In other words, these forces must persist until the entire excess of demand over supply is eliminated. If we start by supposing supply to exceed demand, the converse chain of sequences will operate. Now these very simple steps of reasoning illuminate the nature of the normal equilibrium of demand and supply. They reveal that the equilibrium is established and maintained by the agency of *changes in price,* and they enable us to lay it down as perhaps the most important thing that can be said about the price of anything that it will tend to be such as will equate demand and supply. But that is not all that they reveal. They reveal also the extreme dependence of both demand and supply upon price. Now this is a fact which it is most important to realize vividly. It is apt to be obscured by customary modes of speech. In ordinary times the prices of most commodities and services do not change by very much, unless indeed over a long period of years ; the amounts demanded and supplied may therefore seem to maintain a fairly constant level ; and we may be tempted to speak of Great Britain producing so many million tons of coal, or America consuming so many millions of motor-cars per annum, almost as though these quantities were independent of price considerations. But we should never forget that there is no service or commodity produced by man, however essential it may seem, the demand for or the supply of which might not be reduced to nothing, if the price were sufficiently raised on the one hand, or lowered on the other. How easy it is sometimes to forget this simple truth may be seen from the mistake so commonly made of supposing, because the peoples of Central Europe were left, on the cessation of the war, starving and destitute of the means of life and the materials of work, that they must necessarily become heavy purchasers of imported goods ; without pausing to consider whether the prices were such as they could afford to pay.

§ 2. *Diagrams and their Uses.* It will help to prevent mistakes like this and more generally to make sharp and clear the fundamental relations which exist between demand, supply and price, if we exhibit them pictorially in the form of a diagram. Such diagrams are of great service in many parts of economic theory, not because they can prove anything which could not be proved otherwise, but because, being really a simpler medium of expression than words, they enable the mind to grasp more readily and to retain more vividly the essential facts of complex relations.

In Fig. 1 the curve DD′ represents the conditions of demand. It is supposed to be drawn in such a way that

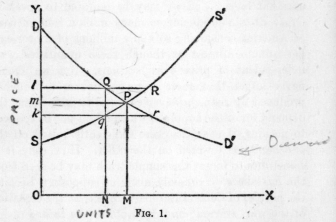

FIG. 1.

if any point, Q, be taken on the curve, and the perpendicular QN be drawn to meet the base line, or axis OX, then ON will represent the amount that will be demanded at a price represented by QN (or O*l*). In other words, distances measured along OY represent prices, and distances measured along OX represent quantities of the commodity, or service, or whatever it may be. Clearly, then, the demand curve, DD′, must slope downwards from left to right, since the lower the price asked, the greater will be the amount demanded.

Similarly the curve SS' represents the conditions of supply. It is supposed to be so drawn that if any point q be taken upon it, and the perpendicular qN be drawn to meet OX, then ON will represent the amount that will be supplied at a price represented by qN (or Ok). Equally clearly this supply curve must slope upwards from left to right, since the higher the price obtainable, the greater will be the quantity offered. Take the point P where the two curves meet, and draw the perpendicular PM to meet OX. Then the third law enunciated at the beginning of this chapter corresponds to the statement that PM or Om will represent the price at which the commodity or service will be exchanged.

It can readily be seen that no other price could be maintained. For suppose the price to be less than Om, suppose it to be Ok, then, at this price, ON (or kq) will be the amount supplied, and kr the amount demanded. The demand will thus exceed the supply, and the price will tend to rise, i.e. to move upwards towards Om. Similarly if we suppose the price to be Ol, which is larger than Om, the supply (lR) will exceed the demand (lQ) and the price will fall downwards towards Om. Thus, again, we have deduced Law III from Laws I and II with the form and precision of a proposition in Euclid. Now, when once the eye has become familiar with this diagram, it ought to be impossible for the mind to lose even momentarily its grip on the fact that demand and supply are both dependent upon price. For these curves do not represent any particular amounts; they represent a series of *relations* between amount and price; if the

price is QN the amount demanded is ON, and so forth.
The terms demand and supply in the sense, in which
I have been using them, of the respective amounts
demanded and supplied are, indeed, strictly meaning-
less without reference to some particular price. The
reference may sometimes be implicit; but, whenever there
is a chance of ambiguity, it should be explicitly made.

§ 3. *Ambiguities of the Expressions, " Increase in
Demand," etc.* It is the more important to be precise
upon this point, in that there is a further possible
confusion which we have now to consider. Demand
and supply, as we have seen, are dependent upon
price ; but equally clearly they are dependent upon
other things as well. Demand depends upon the needs,
tastes and habits of the people, as well as upon the
length of their purse ; supply depends upon such
things as the cost of production in the case of commodities. None of these is a constant factor, all of
them are liable to change, and it may well happen
that we shall want to consider in some concrete problem
the probable consequences of such a change. Now the
most usual and natural way of describing such changes
in the medium of words is to use the expression
" increase " or " decrease in demand," and " increase "
or " decrease in supply," the same expressions, which
we employed before to describe the consequences of a
change in price. This identity of language conceals
a fundamental distinction between the phenomena
described ; and to make this distinction plain we cannot
do better than revert to our diagrammatic presentation
of the laws.

In Fig. 2 we start as before with our demand curve
and supply curve, cutting one another at the point P.
We then suppose that some alteration takes place in
the conditions of demand ; there has been a growth
in the general taste for the commodity or service, and
the demand, as we say, has increased accordingly.

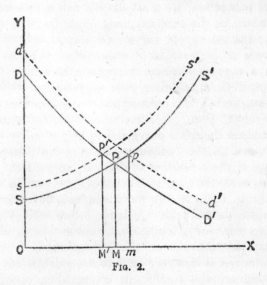

FIG. 2.

How is this fact to be represented in the diagram ?
Plainly not by taking another point on the curve, DD′,
at a further distance from OY. For this would merely
indicate the larger amount that would be taken, if the
conditions of demand had remained unaltered but the
sellers had reduced their prices. The correct way of
representing the change we have supposed is to construct a new demand curve (in the figure, the dotted

curve *dd'*), lying at every point above the old demand curve. For this indicates that larger quantities will be purchased at the old prices, which is exactly what we want to represent. Similarly if we wish to represent a change in the conditions of supply, such as might result, in the case of a commodity, from a tax imposed on its production, we must draw a new supply curve, *ss'*, which in the case supposed, must lie everywhere above the old supply curve. On the other hand, the decrease or increase in demand or supply, *resulting* from a change in price, is represented simply by a shifting of the equilibrium from one point to another on the same curve. The striking pictorial contrast between a movement from one curve to another, and a movement along the same curve should help to make vivid to our minds the fundamental distinction between a change in the *conditions* of demand, arising from new tastes, enhanced purchasing power, etc.; and a mere change in the amount purchased resulting from an alteration in the price which the sellers ask. Words, as this necessarily cumbrous sentence shows, are a clumsy instrument for the expression of abstract relations ; it is not very easy to see which words in a sentence are the significant, commanding ones, and which are performing, as it were, ordinary routine duties. A diagram is not exposed to similar ambiguities of emphasis.

The particular distinction, to which attention has been called, is important. The reader who has grasped it clearly will be able to perceive many instances of the confusion arising out of its neglect in the ordinary discussions of economic questions which take place in the press and on the platform. It is not uncommon, for instance, for an argument to run something like this : " The effect of a tax on this commodity might seem at first sight to be an advance in price. But an advance in price will diminish the demand ; and a reduced demand will send the price down again. It is not certain, therefore, after all, that the tax will really raise the price." A glance at the diagram will keep us out of such a bog of sophistry and muddle. For if we suppose the amount of the tax per unit of the commodity to be represented by Ss, the curve ss' (drawn, as it is, roughly parallel to SS') will represent the new conditions of supply after the tax has been imposed. The new position of equilibrium will be given by the point P', where ss' cuts DD', the demand curve. Now P' lies to the left of P the old point of equilibrium ; hence, since DD' *must* slope downwards from left to right, it is clear that, if, as it is fair here to assume, the *conditions* of demand have remained unaltered, the new price P'M', must be greater than the old.

§ 4. *Reactions of Changes in Demand and Supply on Price.* Having now made clear the meaning that must be attached to the terms, let us consider the question which naturally arises, whether we can lay down any general propositions or laws as to the effect upon price, of an increase or decrease in demand or supply. Another glance at the diagram suggests that we can. An increase in demand is represented in Fig. 2 by a movement from DD' to dd', which cuts the supply curve, SS', at p, to the right of P. Since the supply

curve (drawn, as it is best to draw it, to represent the
amount which will be supplied in response to a given
price) must always slope upwards from left to right,
the new price, *pm*, must be greater than the old, PM.
Conversely a decrease in demand is represented by a
movement from *dd'* to DD', and the new price is
seen to be less than the old. We have already seen
that a decrease in supply, which is represented by a
movement from SS' to *ss'* results in a higher price;
and it is the obvious converse that an increase in
supply will have the opposite effect. It would seem
then that we might lay down quite generally that an
increase in demand or a decrease in supply will raise the
price while a decrease in demand or an increase in
supply will lower it.

But here it is necessary to be cautious. All conclusions as to the effects of causes are necessarily based,
implicitly, if not explicitly, upon the assumption
" other things being equal." This method of reasoning,
which some people appear to find so irritating in the
economic sphere, and as they say so " theoretical "
and " unreal," is one which they adopt readily enough
in every other department of life. No one, for instance,
objects to the statement that the sun, when it comes
out, makes a room warmer, although it may very
well happen, if a fire is dying at the same time, that
the room grows colder in point of fact. For in our
general statement we assume implicitly that " other
things " such as fires, are unchanged. But assumptions
of this kind are legitimate only when there is no reason
to suppose that the cause, the effects of which are
being studied, will itself produce a change in the " other

things." If (as I have often been told ; I really do not know if it is true) the rays of the sun help to put a fire out, the statement made above would be the better for some qualification.

Now we can only say that an increase in demand raises price, if we assume the conditions of supply (as represented by the supply curve) to remain unchanged. But in practice, an increase in demand may cause a change in the *conditions* of supply. An increase, for instance, in the demand for a commodity may give rise to a revolution in the methods of production, to the introduction of labour-saving machinery and so forth, which will eventually result in the commodity being produced more cheaply. It will certainly take a considerable time before reactions of this kind can exert an appreciable influence ; and we can, therefore, feel reasonably sure that over a short period an increase in demand will raise the price. But we cannot be sure what the ultimate effect will be. A similar alteration in the condition of demand is less likely to result from an increase or decrease in supply ; but it may conceivably occur. We must, therefore, be careful to qualify any general propositions which we lay down in this connection, by explicit reference to a short period of time. We can add the following to our body of laws :—

IV. An increase in demand, or a decrease in supply will tend to raise the price for a short period at least. Conversely a decrease in demand, or an increase in supply will tend to lower the price for a short period at least.

This law, like the others, applies to commodities,

services, capital, to anything which can be said, literally, or by analogy, to have a price. "A short period" is, however, a vague expression and, since precision is the hallmark of an important law, we must accord to this one a status inferior to that which the preceding three can rightly claim.

§ 5. *Some paradoxical reactions of price changes on supply.* Let us turn, though, once more to these earlier laws, and with a heightened critical sense let us submit them to the test of the whole gamut of our experience, and see if in any of them we can find the smallest flaw. The first of them will pass through the ordeal—let each reader prove it for himself— unscathed. The second will emerge with a few hairs, as it were, singed. It tells us, for instance, that a rise in price will tend to augment the supply. Now there are some things the supply of which cannot possibly be augmented ; these are the capital resources of nature, of which land is the most important for our present purpose. Land is bought and sold, it commands a price. In a certain sense, it may be said to be possible to increase the supply of land, in response to a rise in price, by drainage and reclamation schemes ; and it will certainly happen that a rise in the price which land can command for any particular purpose will increase the amount which is devoted to that purpose. But, speaking broadly, the supply of land available for purposes of every kind is a fixed unvarying factor, with an inertia which the cajolery of price-changes is powerless to disturb. This is a most important fact, and it gives rise to some peculiar features of the price and rent of land, which we shall have to consider later as a separate problem. It constitutes a limiting case rather than an exception to the general law. But we have not yet done with the reactions of price upon supply. In the case of capital, the nature of those reactions has been much discussed as a highly controversial question. That a rise in the rate of interest will cause some people to save more than before, is generally admitted ; but it is pointed out that the effect upon others may be the exact opposite, because it means that they do not need to save so much to acquire the same future annual income. It is unwise to say dogmatically that the former tendency outweighs the latter ; though upon the whole it seems highly probable that it does. We cannot, therefore, in this case feel confident that a change in price will react upon supply in the manner which our law indicates. Similarly it is possible to argue that a rise in the general level of real wages may reduce the supply of labour, even, or some might say particularly, if the term is used to denote not the number of workpeople, but the quantity of work done. For there may be a tendency for workpeople, when more comfortably off, to work less regularly or less hard. Here again we cannot be sure. In none of these cases, however, including that of land, is there any reason to doubt that a rise in price will diminish *demand*, or conversely that a fall will increase it. Since, therefore, in the reasoning by which we deduced the third law, the conclusion will hold good, even if the effects of price-changes on supply are of the above paradoxical kind, provided that they do not continually outweigh the effects upon demand, there is no reason to cast doubt on the solidity of Law III, which, indeed, as we suggested before, commends itself directly to experience. But Law II seems now, perhaps, somewhat the worse for wear.

The damage, however, is not considerable. For in each case the uncertainty arises only when we are dealing with one of the factors of production, land, labour or capital, *regarded as a whole*. If we are dealing with the capital available for a particular industry, a rise in the rate of profit in that industry will certainly increase the supply of capital available there ; for it will tend to attract savings that might otherwise have been employed elsewhere. We can even be fairly sure that an increase in the general rate of interest prevailing in any particular country will increase the total supply of capital available for the businesses of that country, since capital has in modern times acquired a considerable migratory power. In the case of labour, we cannot go so far as this ; but here, too, there is no doubt that an increase in the renumeration offered in any particular occupation will attract an increased labour supply (always supposing, of course, that " other things are equal "). No similar difficulty arises for land, labour or capital, as regards the effect of price-changes on demand ; while for ordinary commodities there is no such difficulty on the side either of demand or of supply. Hence the only qualification which the strictest accuracy would require us in this connection to attach to our statement of Law II is the postscript :—

"Except that, in the case of land, the aggregate supply is unalterable ; while in the case of capital or labour we cannot be sure how price-changes will affect the aggregate supply."

Much significance attaches to these exceptions, as later will appear.

§ 6. *The Disturbances of Monetary Changes.* But let us still keep a critical eye on Law II, and submit it to another flashlight from our practical experience. The recent world war made us all acutely aware of a remarkable rise in the price of almost everything, which yet did not seem to diminish appreciably the demand. The explanation of this paradox is not difficult to find. There was an immense increase in the volume of nominal purchasing power, due to a complex set of causes, of which " currency inflation " may be taken as the symbol. Now perhaps we are entitled to assume the absence of such currency changes as part of the " other things being equal " which is always understood as implied. But it is rash to take this particular assumption for granted, for many people, having only a vague and intermittent understanding of monetary matters, are inclined to suppose that there is something natural and normal about a price level which has been long established. It would be safer, therefore, to add explicitly to Law II the reservation, " Assuming that there is no change in the general volume of purchasing power."

Monetary and allied questions form the subject of another volume of this series. It must not be supposed that our general laws have no bearing on them. On the contrary, Law I, which all this time has remained serene and undisturbed by the occasional discomfitures of Law II, is the gateway through which all questions of currency, banking and the foreign exchanges should be approached. It is well to note, as an inexorable corollary of Law I, that prices can rise *only* if demand exceeds supply, and fall *only* if supply exceeds demand ; and hence that it is only through the agency of changes in the demand for and supply of commodities and services that an inflation or deflation of the currency can influence the price level. Further, since a condition of things in which supply generally exceeds demand spells what we know and fear as a trade depression, it may be well to note at once that falling prices and unemployment are inseparable bedfellows. For we are far too apt to shut our eyes to these unpleasant truths. But we cannot pursue them further here ; and in the remainder of this volume we shall not be concerned (except, perhaps, incidentally) with questions affecting the general level of prices or of purchasing power ; but rather with the relation which the price of one commodity bears to that of another, with the rate of interest (which being a rate per cent is not essentially dependent on the price level), with " real " wages (as distinct from money wages) and the like.

§ 7. *The Trade Cycle.* But our reference to trade depressions suggests a final comment on Law II. One small qualification was embodied in our original statement of it, namely the words "sooner or later." A rise in price may not check the demand immediately (even if the printing presses are standing idle in the Treasuries); it may actually stimulate it for a time. For people may fear that the price will rise further still, and hasten to buy what they *must* buy before very long. Sellers may share the same opinion, and be reluctant on their side to part. When prices are falling the rôles are reversed, and we are likely to see the sellers tumbling over one another in a frantic eagerness to sell, the buyers wary and aloof. Sooner or later, indeed, these tendencies must dissolve and disappear ; but they may persist for a longer period than might seem probable at first. For the raw material of one trade is, as we say, the finished product of another. The demand for one thing gives rise to a demand for other things, for the labour with which to make them, and so on in an expanding circle. A sympathy, subtle and intense, unites the business world, and a wave of depression or animation arising in any quarter may spread itself far and wide, heightened by the gusts of human hope and fear, and continue long before its influence is spent.

Here we are upon the threshold of one of the most striking and formidable of economic facts, the regular alternation of periods of good and bad trade, each very widespread, if not world-wide, in its range, each comprising certain regular phases of acceleration and decay, and each infallibly yielding sooner or later to the other. The details of these phenomena are highly complex, some of them obscure ; an immense literature has already been devoted to the subject, yet its systematic study is hardly more than begun. The account given in the preceding paragraph is incomplete and meagre. It is inserted here in the hope that it will impress the reader with a sense both of the fact of these alternations and of the deeply rooted nature of the causes from which they spring. They take a heavy toll of human happiness and wealth ; and there is no object that more urgently calls for concerted human effort than that of mitigating

D

them, and of alleviating the misery which they bring in their train. Still better, of eradicating them if that is possible ; but let none suppose that it can be lightly done. Meanwhile, let us always remember that they form the atmosphere and medium in which the enduring tendencies of the business world must work themselves out. It is often convenient to speak of "normal conditions" in this trade or that ; but hardly ever can it be truly said of a particular moment that conditions are normal. The normal is rather a mean level about which oscillations to and fro, round and about, are constantly taking place, but which itself is reached only by accident, if at all. Whenever we say that some new factor should in the long run lower the price of this or that commodity or service, the picture which these words should convey to our mind is one of the price rising less in times of boom, and falling more in times of depression than is the case with other things. And if ever our faith in some honoured economic law is shaken by the apparent ease with which, perhaps, in times of active trade, sellers are able to advance their prices to whatever figure (so it almost seems) they choose to name, or by the persistence with which in times of depression supply exceeds demand for almost every commodity and service, let us rally our sense of economic rhythm, and reserve our judgment until the trade cycle has run its course.

CHAPTER III

UTILITY AND THE MARGIN OF CONSUMPTION

§ 1. *The Forces behind Supply and Demand.* The laws enunciated in the preceding chapter constitute the framework and skeleton of all economic analysis; but they do not carry us very far. It is only through the agency of these laws that any influence can affect the price of anything : but what influences may so affect it is a question which we have still to consider.

Let us begin with ordinary commodities and ask ourselves, in the light of experience and common sense, upon what factors their price seems mainly to depend ? Two factors spring to mind at once ; their cost of production and their usefulness. As regards the former, the case seems clear enough. We may indeed sometimes grumble that the price of this or that commodity is unconscionably high in comparison with its cost ; but this only goes to show that we conceive a relation between price and cost as the normal, governing rule. If one commodity cost only a half as much to produce as another, we should think that something had gone very wrong indeed, if the former commodity were sold for the higher price. But, when we turn to the usefulness of commodities, the case is not so clear. Usefulness has

37

some connection with price, so much is certain; for an entirely useless thing, fit only for the dust-bin (and known to be such, it may be well to add) will fetch no price at all, however costly it may be to produce. But it is not easy to express the connection in quantitative terms. It seems reasonable enough to say that the prices of commodities are roughly proportionate to their costs of production. But directly we contemplate saying a similar thing of their usefulness, we are pulled up short. As we look round the world, and enumerate the commodities which by common consent are the most useful, salt, water, bread, and so forth, the striking paradox presents itself that these are among the cheapest of all commodities; far cheaper than champagne, motor-cars or ball dresses, which we could very well get on without. As things are, of course, a ball dress, or a motor-car costs more to produce than a loaf of bread or a packet of salt; and the common-sense explanation of the paradox seems, therefore, to be that the cost of production is a more weighty influence than the usefulness, or utility, as we will henceforth call it (so as to include the satisfaction we derive from not strictly useful things). We are thus tempted to conclude that, provided a commodity possesses some utility, its price will be determined by the cost of production, the degree of utility being unimportant. This was exactly how the position was summed up for many years in systematic treatises upon Political Economy; and it was not until fully half a century after the *Wealth of Nations* that a discovery was made which threw a fresh light on the whole matter.

First of all, let it be clearly observed how very

unsatisfactory is the above account. In Chapter II, where we were treading surely, with a sense of solid ground beneath us, we drew no such invidious distinction between supply and demand. They seemed then to possess an equal status. But cost of production is the chief factor which, in the case of commodities, ultimately determines the conditions of supply. Utility, similarly, is the chief factor which ultimately determines the conditions of demand. Must not then the symmetrical relations between demand and supply be reflected in a corresponding symmetry between the utility and the costs which underlie them ? Demand springs obviously from utility ; the only motive for buying anything is that it will serve some real or fancied use. Can we then accord to demand so dignified and to utility so subordinate a place ? There is here an inconsistency which we must somehow reconcile. It will not serve as a solution to distinguish between different periods of time, and to say, as economists used to say not very long ago, that price is governed over a short period by demand and supply, but in the long run by the cost of production. This still leaves our sense of symmetry unsatisfied. Moreover, the conception of cost of production, when we consider it as ruling over a long period, frequently seems to lose any precision, as an independent factor, which it may otherwise possess. Motor-cars, we have agreed, are more costly to produce than loaves of bread ; but, as we know well, the cost of producing motor-cars varies enormously, accordingly as they are produced on a small or a large scale. By the methods of mass production they can be turned out at a relatively low cost per car. But this requires that they should be purchased in large numbers ; and this in turn throws us back to the demand for motor-cars, and plainly enough, to people's judgment as to their utility.   In some cases, the opposite phenomenon occurs, In the case of British coal, for instance, the average cost of production would be much lower than it is if the output were reduced to a fraction of its present volume, and if only the richer seams of the more fertile mines were worked.   Once again, therefore, it is difficult to measure the cost of production until we know the magnitude of the demand, which in a manner, which we have still to elucidate, clearly depends upon the utility.

If we take the problem of joint products, the conception of cost of production fails us still more conspicuously.   For what is the cost of producing wool, or the cost of producing mutton ?   We can speak of the cost of rearing sheep : but it is hardly possible to allot this cost, except quite arbitrarily, between the two products.   How, then, can we explain the separate prices of these things by reference to cost alone ? Instances of joint production are becoming so common in the modern world, or at least, with the growing attention to the utilization of by-products, are assuming so much more heightened a significance, that an explanation of price, which does not apply to them, is a very feeble one indeed.

§ 2.   *The Law of Diminishing Utility*.   Let us turn back, then, to the factor of utility, and see if we cannot put on a more satisfactory basis the relation between utility and price.   The clue to the puzzle is to be found

in a brief reflection on the implications of the second
general law propounded in Chapter II. A rise in price,
it was there stated, will sooner or later diminish the
demand. This was asserted as a matter of fact, observed
from and confirmed by experience. But what does it
signify ? To what causes is this familiar fact to be
attributed ? The first stage of the answer is very
simple. The many individuals, whose purchases make
up the demand for the commodity, will buy smaller
quantities now that the price is higher. Possibly some
of them may cease to buy it altogether; but as a rule
it would be reasonable to suppose that most people continue to buy a certain amount though a smaller amount
than hitherto. Let us turn our attention, then, to the
individual purchaser, and ask ourselves why he (or let
us say she) acts in the manner indicated. The obvious
answer is that the more she already has of anything,
the less urgently does she require a little more of it.
If she buys 6 lb. of sugar every week when the price is
7d a lb, but only 5 lb. when the price is 8d, she shows
by her action that she does not consider that the
additional utility she will derive from buying 6 lb. a
week rather than 5 lb. is worth as much as 8d. But she
shows at the same time that she thinks it worth 7d.
For, when the price is 7d, no one compels her to buy that
sixth pound. She could stop, if she chose, at five ; and
it may serve to make the point quite plain if we suppose
her actually to hesitate before she buys the sixth.
She has hitherto, let us say, been buying 5 lb. a week
at 8d a lb. To-day she enters the shop and finds the
price is down to 7d. She asks for her customary 5 lb. ;
then she pauses, and a minute later turns her order into

six. What are the alternatives which she has been weighing one against the other in that momentary pause ? Not the utility of the whole 6 lb. of sugar against the total price of 42d. For she has already ordered the first 5 lb. ; and the decision to buy the sixth is taken independently and subsequently. She has been sizing up the *increment* of utility which a sixth pound would yield, and she decides that this is worth the expenditure of a further 7d. Again, when the price was 8d she need not have bought as many as 5 lbs. She could have stopped at 4 had she chosen, and the fact that she did buy 5 lb. shows that the increment of utility derived from buying a fifth pound, when she might be said already to have 4, was worth at least 8d in her judgment.

This trite illustration enables us to lay down two important laws relating to utility. To state them shortly, it is convenient to employ one or two technical terms, which, unlike every term employed hitherto, are not very commonly used in their present sense in everyday life. Their adoption is desirable not merely for the sake of convenience, but because they help to stamp clearly on the mind a most illuminating conception, that of the " margin," which supplies the clue to many complicated problems. The last pound of sugar which the housewife purchased, the fifth pound when the price was 8d, or the sixth pound when the price was 7d, we call the " marginal " pound of sugar. And the increment of utility which she derives from buying this marginal pound we call the " marginal utility " of sugar to her. We are thus able to state the fact that the more a person has of anything the less urgently does he require a little more of it, in the following formal terms :—

V. The marginal utility of a commodity to anyone diminishes with every increase in the amount he has.

The total utility will, of course, increase with an increase in the amount, but at a diminishing rate. This law is usually called The Law of Diminishing Utility.

§ 3. *Relation between Price and Marginal Utility.* But this is not all. We are now in a position to perceive the true relation between utility and price. The relation is one which exists not between price and total utility, but between price and marginal utility. If we know only that a housewife will buy weekly 5 lb. of sugar at 8d per lb., but 6 lb. at 7d, we know nothing of the total utility of sugar to her. We do not know how much she might be prepared to pay rather than go without 3 lb., 2 lb., or any sugar at all. But we do know that, when she buys 6 lb., the marginal utility of sugar is in her judgment worth something which does not differ greatly from the price. We can, therefore, say in general terms that the price of a commodity measures approximately its marginal utility to the purchaser.

This statement is perfectly consistent with the paradox noted above that the most useful commodities such as bread, salt and water are very cheap. For when we say that these commodities are supremely useful, we mean only that their total utility is very great ; that, rather than do without them altogether, we would offer for them a large proportion of our means.

But we would not value very highly a small addition to the bread, water or salt that we habitually consume ; nor would most of us feel it as a very serious deprivation if our consumption of these things were curtailed by a small percentage. In other words, their *marginal* utilities are small, and it is only the *marginal* utility that has any relation to price.

§ 4. *The Marginal Purchaser.* A possible objection to the preceding argument deserves to be considered. Some readers may find the picture I have drawn of the hesitating housewife entirely unconvincing. They may declare that her mind does not work at all in the manner I have indicated. She will have formed certain habits in regard to her weekly purchases of sugar, which are connected very vaguely, if at all, with any conscious processes of thought. She will buy so many pounds of sugar weekly without troubling her head over the specific utility of the last pound she buys. When the price falls she may, indeed, buy more ; but it will not be because she separates out and considers by itself the extra utility of an additional pound. She may buy more, because she has formed the habit of spending so much money on sugar ; and now that the price has fallen, the same amount of money will enable her to buy more pounds. Or, perhaps, she may be moved by instinctive and irresistible attraction to buy more of a thing when it is cheaper, similar to that which inspires so many people to face with ardour the horrors of a bargain sale. In any case the fine calculations I have imagined convey a fantastic picture of her state of mind. And how much more fantastic, the critic may

continue, of the state of mind in which things of a
different kind are bought by less careful people. When,
for instance, one of us happy-go-lucky males (more
liberally supplied, perhaps, than the housewife with the
necessary cash), decides to buy a motor bicycle, or to
replenish his stock of collars or ties, does the above
analysis bear any resemblance to the actual facts ? In
the case of the motor bicycle, the purchaser may, indeed,
weigh the price fairly carefully against the pleasure and
benefit, though contrariwise he may be a rich enough
gentleman hardly to bother about this. But, one motor
bicycle is as much as he is at all likely to buy, and what
becomes, then, of the distinction between total and
marginal utility ? In the case of the ties and collars,
the vagueness of many of us about the price will
be extreme. We probably have been uneasily conscious
for some time of an inconvenient shortage of these
troublesome articles and eventually will go off (or
perhaps will be sent off with ignominy) to the nearest
suitable shop to make good the deficiency. How can
we speak here with a straight face of the relation
between marginal utility and price ?

These are very pertinent criticisms ; but they do
not make nearly as much nonsense of the notion of
marginal utility as may seem at first. The last
point, indeed, serves rather to give it a fresh aspect
of much significance. Those of us who do not bother
about the price we pay for our ties and collars owe a
debt of gratitude, of which we are insufficiently conscious,
to the more careful people who do ; as well as to the
custom which prevails in shops in Western countries
(as distinct from the bazaars of the East) of charging

as a rule a uniform price to all customers. If *we* were the only people who bought these things, an enterprising salesman would be able to charge us very much what he chose. He could put up his price, and we would hardly be aware of it. And, as by lowering his price he could not tempt us to buy any more, price reductions would be few and far between. But fortunately there are always some people who do know what the price is, even when they are buying collars and ties ; and who will adjust the amount they buy in accordance with the price. It is these worthy people who make the laws of demand work out as we well know they do. It is they who will curtail their consumption if the price has risen and it is they who constitute the seller's problem, and help to keep down prices for the rest of us. The rest of us—it is well to be quite blunt about it—simply do not count in this connection. We have no cause then to plume ourselves that we have disproved the truth of economic laws when we declare that we seldom weigh the utility of anything against its price. All that this shows is that our actions are too insignificant to be described by economic laws since they exert no appreciable influence on the price of anything. And this in turn shows the extreme importance of grasping clearly the conception of the margin. Just as it is the marginal purchase, so it is the marginal purchaser who matters. It is the man who, before he buys a motor bicycle, weighs the matter up very carefully indeed and only just decides to buy it, who is the really note-worthy figure among the purchasers of motor bicycles. It is the utility which *he* derives that constitutes the marginal utility, which is roughly measured by the price.

As to the housewife, I am not prepared to concede that my picture is in essentials very fanciful. She may be a creature of habits and instincts like the rest of us, but most habits and instincts affecting household expenditure are based ultimately on *some* calculation, if not one's own, and reason has a way of paying, as it were, periodic visits of inspection, and pulling our habits and instincts into line, if they have gone far astray. I am not satisfied that the housewife does not envisage the utility of a sixth pound of sugar as something distinct from the utility of the other five ; she may buy it, for example, with the definite object of giving the children some sugar on their bread, and she may have a very clear idea as to the price which sugar must not exceed before she will do any such thing. Possibly I exaggerate. I have the profound respect of the incorrigibly wasteful male for the care and skill she displays in laying out her money to the best advantage.

§ 5. *The Business Man as Purchaser*. But if the reader still finds the picture unconvincing, let us shift the scene from domestic economy to commerce, and substitute for the careful housewife an enterprising business man. Now, as anyone who has a business man for his father will have often heard him say, the vagueness and caprice which characterize our personal expenditure would be quire intolerable in business affairs. There you must weigh and measure with the utmost possible precision. You must be for ever watching the several channels of your expenditure, careful to see that in none does the stream rise higher than the level at which further expenditure ceases to be profitable. You will not even engage typists or instal a telephone in your office without weighing up fairly carefully the number of typists or the number of switches that it is worth your while to have. And in deciding whether to employ, say, five typists, or six, you will not vaguely lump the services of the whole six typists together, and consider whether as a whole they are worth to you the wages you must give them. You will, in the most direct and literal manner, weigh up the *additional* benefit you would derive from a sixth typist, and if that does not seem to you equivalent to her wage, you will not engage her, however essential it may be to you to have one or two typists in your office. If on the other hand, the utility of having a sixth typist seems to you worth much more than her pay, the chances are that you will be well advised to consider the employment of a seventh. And so, where you stop employing further typists, the utility to you of the last one, of the " marginal typist " as it were, is unlikely to differ greatly from her pay.

Now this is not a fancy picture of some remote abstraction called an " economic man." Allowing for the over-emphasis which is necessary to drive home the central point, it is a bald account of the aims and methods of the actual man of business. To ascertain the margin of profitable expenditure in each direction, to go thus and no further, is the very essence of the business spirit, as the business man himself conceives it. When he condemns the extravagance of Government departments, it is their lack of just this marginal sense that he chiefly has in mind. " The lore of nicely calculated less or more " may be rejected by High Heaven and Whitehall, but no one can afford to despise it in the business world.

The transition from household to business expenditure involves an extended use of the word utility, which is worth noting. Commodities like bread, sugar, or privately owned motor-cars are sometimes called "consumers' goods" in contrast to "producers' goods," which comprise things such as raw materials, machinery, the services of typists and so forth, which are bought by business men for business purposes. The line of division between the two classes is not a sharp one, and we need not trouble with fine-spun questions as to whether a particular commodity should in certain circumstances be included under the one head or the other. But, broadly speaking, things of the former type yield a direct utility ; they contribute directly to the satisfaction of our pleasures or our wants. Things of the latter type yield rather an indirect utility. Their utility to the business man who buys them lies in the assistance they give him in making something else from which he will derive a profit. The utility of these things is therefore said to be *derived* from that of the consumers' goods or services to which they ultimately contribute. This conception of derived utility leads to certain complications which we shall have to notice later.

§ 6. *The Diminishing Utility of Money.* But one important point must be emphasized in this chapter. The utility which a business man derives from the things which he buys for business purposes is the extra receipts which he obtains thereby. Derived utility, in other words, is expressed in terms of money, and the idea of its relation to price presents no difficulty. But the utility of things which are bought for personal consumption means the *satisfaction* which they yield, and this is clearly not a thing which is commensurable with money. When, therefore, it is said that the prices measure their respective marginal utilities, what exactly is meant? What was it that the argument of § 3 went to show? That the utility of the marginal pound of sugar would seem to the housewife just worth the price that she must pay for it; in other words, that it would be roughly equal to the utility she could obtain by spending the money in other ways. The respective marginal utilities which *she* obtains from the different things she buys will thus be proportionate to their prices. But if she were to receive a legacy which gave her a much larger income to spend, she might buy larger quantities of practically every commodity; and, though she would obtain a greater total utility thereby, the marginal utility she would obtain in each direction would be smaller, in accordance with the law of diminishing utility. The prices might not have changed; the respective marginal utilities to her of the different things would again be proportionate to their prices, but they would constitute a smaller satisfaction than before.

Thus we can only say that the prices of commodities will be proportionate to their real marginal utilities, when we are considering the different purchases of one and the same individual. The amounts of money which different people are prepared to pay for

different consumers' goods are no reliable indication
of the real utilities, the amounts of human satisfaction
which they yield. Here we must take account not
only of varying needs and capacities for enjoyment,
but of the very unequal manner in which purchasing
power is distributed among the people. The cigars
which a rich man may buy will yield him an immeasurably smaller satisfaction than that which a poor family
could obtain by spending the same amount of money
on boots, or clothes or milk. When, therefore, we
compare commodities which are bought by essentially
different consuming publics, their respective prices may
bear no close relation to their *real* utility, whether
marginal or otherwise. Thus the law of diminishing
utility applies to money or purchasing power, as well
as to particular commodities. The more money a
man has the less is the marginal utility which it yields
him ; and, where the marginal utility of money to a
man is small, so also will be the real marginal utility
he derives in each direction of his expenditure. The
extreme inequality of the distribution of wealth gives
immense importance to this consideration. Its practical
implications will be discussed in Chapter V. Meanwhile,
we may express the conclusions of the present chapter
by the statement that the price of a commodity tends
to equal its marginal utility, *as measured in terms of
money*, i.e. relatively to the marginal utility of money
to its purchaser.

E

CHAPTER IV

COST AND THE MARGIN OF PRODUCTION

§ 1. *An Illustration from Coal.* We have already had occasion to note the symmetry which characterizes the relations of demand and supply to price. This symmetry was apparent throughout the argument of Chapter II, and it was a striking feature of the diagrams which we employed to illustrate the argument. We shall do well to cultivate a lively sense of this symmetry, for it will frequently save us from ignoring factors which have a vital bearing on the problems we are considering. We should never leave an important feature of demand without turning to see whether it has a counterpart on the supply side, though indeed we may not always find one. In the last chapter we examined the relation between utility and price, and found that the true relation was between the price and what we termed the marginal utility. Corresponding to utility on the demand side is cost of production on the supply side. The question should thus at once suggest itself—" Can we speak appropriately of a marginal cost of production, and will this serve to make clearer the relation between cost and price ? " To answer these questions, let us take one of the instances in which we found that price could not be explained satisfactorily by the bare phrase "cost of production."

An important feature of the coal industry, which recent events have brought into sharp prominence, is the great diversity of conditions between different coalfields and different collieries. We speak of rich seams and poor seams, of fertile and unfertile mines, and we are aware that the costs of raising coal to the surface differ very widely in accordance with these diverse natural conditions. Nor must we confine our attention to the cost price at the pit-head. If we wish to speak of cost of production as a factor determining price, we must use the term in a broad sense to include the transport and other charges necessary to bring the coal to market.

In this respect also one coalfield differs greatly from another. Some are well situated close to a large market, or within easy reach of the seaboard; others must incur very heavy transport charges to bring their coal to any considerable centre of consumption. These varying conditions lead, as we well know, to great variations in the financial prosperity of different colliery concerns. In Great Britain, under the abnormal conditions which prevailed during the war, and subsequently, these variations were so huge as to constitute a most formidable embarrassment and to contribute, more perhaps than any other single factor, to the unrest and instability by which the industry has been afflicted. But they are always with us, if usually upon a more modest scale.

What, then, is the normal relation between price and cost in the case of coal? Should we direct our attention to the average costs over the whole industry, or the costs incurred by the richer and better situated mines, or, lastly, that of the poorer and worse situated ? Now, as things are, it is clear enough that no concern will continue indefinitely producing at a loss. It may do so for a time, rather than close down altogether, hoping to recoup itself later when the market has taken a more favourable turn. But, in the long run, taking good years with bad, it must expect to obtain receipts sufficient not only to cover its necessary expenditure, but to provide also a reasonable profit on the capital employed. Of course, once the capital has been sunk and embodied in plant and buildings, which are of little use for any other purpose, a business may continue for many years, with a rate of profit far below what it had anticipated. But plant and buildings gradually wear out, and need to be replaced ; the course of technical improvement calls continually for fresh capital outlay, which a business in a bad way is reluctant to undertake. The tendency, therefore, when profits rule low over a considerable period, is for the plant to fall gradually into disrepair and obsolescence, and finally for the business to disappear. We can thus include an ordinary rate of profit under the head of cost of production, and say with substantial accuracy that for no business can this cost for long exceed the price if the business is to continue to exist. If then the relatively poor and badly situated mines are to be worked, the price of coal, taking good years together with bad, must cover the costs at which these mines can produce. If the price rules lower than this, sooner or later they will close down, and we will be left

with a smaller number of mines, among which great
variations of conditions will still prevail. Once more,
the price must cover the cost incurred by the least
profitable of these remaining mines, unless their number
is still further to be diminished. Thus we can conceive
of a "margin of production" which will shift backwards
to more profitable or forwards to include less profitable
mines, according as the demand for coal contracts
or expands. But, wherever this margin may be, there
is no escaping the conclusion that it is the cost of
production of the " marginal mines," of those that is
to say which it is only just worth while to work, to
which the price of coal will approximate.

It follows that there is no real connection between
price and cost of production throughout the industry
as a whole. It follows incidentally that those concerns
which can market their coal at an appreciably lower
cost than the marginal concerns, are likely to reap
more than an ordinary rate of profit, though royalties
may absorb part of the excess.

§ 2. *The Various Aspects of Marginal Cost.* This
relation cuts much deeper than the particular system
under which the mines are at present owned and worked.
If, for instance, we supposed that the various mines
were amalgamated together in a few giant concerns,
each of which comprised some of the richer and some
of the poorer mines, the preceding argument would
need to be recast in form, but its substance would be
unaffected. For though a great coal trust could in a
sense *afford* to sell at a price lower than the marginal
cost, setting its losses on the poorer against its gains

on the better pits, is it likely it would do so ? Why should it dissipate its profits in this way ? It is clearly more reasonable to suppose that it would close down the poorer pits (unless it could advance the price of coal), and thereby maintain its profits at a higher figure. If, indeed, the mines were nationalized the deliberate policy might be pursued of selling coal at a price which left the industry no more than self-supporting as a whole. Some coal might thus be sold at less than its cost price, and the selling price would conform roughly to the *average* cost. But such a policy, though in special circumstances it might be justified, would represent a very dangerous principle, which could not be applied widely without the most serious results. Nothing could be more fatal to any enterprise, whether it be in the hands of an individual, a joint-stock company, a State department, or a Guild, than that the management should content themselves with results which in the lump seem satisfactory, and regard losses here or there with an indifferent eye. That way lies stagnation, waste, progressive inefficiency and ultimate disaster. To enquire searchingly into every nook and cranny of the business, to construct, as it were, for each part a separate balance-sheet of profit and loss, to expand in those directions where further development promises good results, and to curtail activity where loss is already evident, is the very essence of good management. Here, it will be observed, we are using language very similar to that in which we described the principles which govern a business man's expenditure. The resemblance is inevitable and significant, for we are dealing here with what is essentially another aspect of the same thing. The object is to secure that nowhere does expenditure fail to yield a commensurate return. This we express, when we consider a business in its aspect as a consumer, by saying that its consumption of anything will not be carried beyond the point at which the marginal utility exceeds the price it will have to pay. When we consider it as a producer, we say that its production of anything will not be carried beyond the point at which the marginal cost exceeds the price it will obtain.

§ 3. *The Dangers of Ignoring the Margin.* This at least is the general rule. A business may decide deliberately to sell part of its output below cost, because, for instance, this will serve as an advertisement, bring it connections, and enable it to obtain a larger profit at a later date, or immediately on other portions of its sales. In so acting, it recognizes that the price obtained for a thing may be an inadequate measure of the real return it yields. In the same way, though for different reasons, a nationalized coal industry might conceivably be justified in selling some coal below cost price, because, let us say, it held that the price which the immediate purchasers were willing to pay was an inadequate measure of the utility of coal to the community as a whole. But in all such cases it is essential to be very clear as to what exactly you are doing ; so that you may be at least moderately clear as to whether the policy is well advised   It may be sound enough to lose on the swings and make good this loss on the roundabouts, but only if your loss on the swings *helps* you to a larger profit on the roundabouts. If you would get the same return on the roundabouts in any case, it would be better to cut the swings out altogether. So, if you are directing the policy of a nationalized coal industry, and decide to make a loss on a portion of your sales, you will need to know that the indirect benefit which the community will derive from this particular part of your coal output is worth the loss which you incur. You will certainly come to grief, if you pursue a vague ideal of lumping all results together, and regarding a profit somewhere as a sufficient excuse or a positive reason for making a loss elsewhere.

It is quite true that in big undertakings, where there are large standing charges, and where the organization possesses some of the characteristics of an integral whole, it is not easy to measure accurately the specific costs which should be assigned to any particular portion of the output. But this difficulty is one of the most serious weaknesses of large undertakings ; precise detailed measurement is the great prophylactic of business efficiency, and, where it is lacking the bacilli of waste will enter in and multiply. So clearly is this recognized, that the development of large scale business has led to the evolution of new methods of accountancy, designed to make detailed mensuration possible. We have most of us heard of them vaguely under such names as " comparative costings," but too few of us appreciate their full significance. It is hardly too much to say that the issue as to whether the size of the typical business unit will continue to become larger and larger, or whether it has already overshot the point of maximum efficiency will turn largely upon the capacity of accountancy to supply large and complex undertakings with more accurate instruments of detailed financial measurement.

§ 4. *A Misinterpretation.* The price, then, of a com-modity tends roughly to equal its marginal cost of production ; and this marginal cost (in perfect symmetry with what we observed as regards marginal utility), may be conceived as applying either to the marginal producer or to the marginal output of any producer. In the former aspect it is open to a mis-interpretation, against which it will be well to guard. Some advocates of socialism have argued, as one of the counts in their indictment of the present industrial system, that the price of a commodity is determined by the cost at which the least efficient concern in the industry can produce. They say, in effect, " Under the present competitive régime, you have to pay for everything you buy a price which far exceeds the necessary cost to a concern which is managed with ordinary ability. For, as economic theory has shown, it is the cost of the *marginal* concern, i.e. the concern managed by the most incompetent and half-witted fellow in the trade ; it is the cost incurred by him, together with a profit on his capital, that the price has got to cover. The producer of no more than average capacity is therefore making out of you a surplus profit, which would be quite unnecessary in any well-arranged society." Such an argument is a gross caricature of the marginal conception. The half-witted incompetent will, as we know well enough, speedily disappear under the stress of competition, and his place will be taken by more efficient men. There is an essential difference

between him and the "marginal coal mine" of which
we spoke above. For the probabilities are that of the
coal resources, whose existence is clearly known, the
more fertile and better situated parts will already be in
process of exploitation ; and there is not likely, therefore, to be a supply of substantially better seams which
can be substituted for the worst of those in actual use.
There *is* likely, on the other hand, to be available a
supply of decent business capacity which can be substituted for the most inefficient of existing business men.
The marginal concern, in other words, must be conceived as that working under the least advantageous
conditions in respect of the assistance it derives from
the strictly limited resources of nature, but under
average conditions as regards managerial capacity and
human qualities in general. Thus in agriculture we can
speak of a marginal farm, which we should conceive as
the least fertile and worst situated farm which it is just
worth while to cultivate (of which more will be said
when we come to the phenomenon of rent), but we
must assume it to be cultivated by a farmer of average
ability.

§ 5. *Some Consequences of Changes in the Price Level.*
The foregoing controversy will be of service to us, if it
makes clear the manner and the spirit in which the
marginal conception should be handled. It should be
regarded not as a rigid formula which we can apply
to diverse problems without considering the special
features they present, but rather as a signpost which
will enable us to find our way, a compass by which we
may steer between the shoals of triviality and sophistry

to the crux of any problem with which we have to deal. Let us illustrate its practical uses by an example which is of considerable intrinsic importance. While many commodities are normally consumed fairly quickly after they are produced, others last and retain their economic utility for a period of many years. This is true, for example, of houses. It is also true of the instruments of production, factories, machinery, ships and so forth, which constitute our fixed industrial capital. At any particular moment, it is true that the greater part of the existing stock of such things as houses, factories and ships was produced many years ago. Now we can regard the marginal costs of production of such things as being the costs at which additional supplies of them can be produced at the present time, as distinct from the average costs at which the existing stock was produced at different periods in the past. Thus the marginal conception suggests to us that we must not expect the value of a durable commodity, like a house or a factory, to correspond at all closely to the sum which it actually cost to produce it some time ago. It is likely to correspond more closely to the cost of reproducing it, which may be a very different thing.

The costs of production of durable commodities may change for many reasons. It may be instructive to follow out one particular type of change, namely that which arises from changes in the value of money. When, as happened during the war and immediately after-wards, a big increase takes place in the general level of prices and money incomes, the costs of production (reckoned in terms of money) of durable commodities

like factories and machinery are increased in common
with the costs of production of all other commodities.
It will only pay to erect new factories in any industry,
after the price-level has risen, if the profits obtainable
in that industry represent a reasonable return upon the
capital required to construct them at the increased
level of costs.   But such profits will represent, speaking
generally, a high rate of return on the capital spent in
constructing similar factories before the rise in the
price-level occurred.   Thus, except in stagnant or
declining industries, the tendency will be for profits
to rule high upon old capital for some years after a big
rise in the general level of prices has taken place, though
this tendency will gradually disappear as the march of
technical improvement renders the old capital instruments obsolete. Conversely, when a big fall takes place
in the general level of prices, so that the money cost
of building factories and machinery is reduced, there is
likely to be a permanent reduction in the profits which
can be earned by existing capital instruments con-
structed at the higher level of money costs.

These phenomena relating to fixed capital are the
counterpart of similar phenomena relating to circulating
capital which are more generally recognised.   While
prices are actually rising, profits necessarily rule high,
because every trader and manufacturer is constantly
in the position of selling at a higher price-level stock
which he purchased, or goods made from materials
which he purchased, at a lower level. Conversely, when
prices are falling, business men incur losses upon their
stocks. Thus rising (or falling) prices entail abnormal
profits (or losses) upon circulating capital analogous to

the abnormally high (or low) rate of profit which can be earned upon fixed capital. The only difference is that the profits or losses upon circulating capital are crowded into the years when prices are rising or falling, and are thus very noticeable, while the altered profit upon fixed capital accrues in instalments for many years afterwards and may be obscured by the operation of other factors.

Taken together, these two sets of phenomena are of far-reaching significance. They signify that the value of existing capital instruments, and the profits which can be earned upon them, tend to move upwards or downwards along with, and in rough proportion to, the general level of prices. It follows that even large changes in the value of money do not alter very materially the share of profits in the distribution of wealth. That is why an unlimited inflation of the currency makes a less fundamental change in the distribution of wealth than it seems natural to expect. Unlimited inflation is, indeed, fatal to the interests of the *rentier*, to the holder of fixed-interest claims, such as Government loans and debentures ; but, for the most part, what the *rentier* loses the holders of ordinary shares, the owners of the equities of businesses, gain. In times of inflation, accordingly, complaints about " profiteering " are widespread. Conversely, a severe deflation may be very injurious to the holders of ordinary shares, but is correspondingly beneficial to the *rentier*. In times of deflation, accordingly, it is common to hear complaints of the oppressive burden of fixed-interest charges on the productive elements of the community. In both cases, the principal change in

the distribution of real income that is taking place
is a transference from one section of capitalists to
another. The share of the aggregate real income
which capital, as a whole, receives is not radically
changed. This suggests that the distribution of wealth
between the different agents of production is governed
by laws which it is less easy to modify than might
at first sight appear.

We are not yet ready, however, to consider the distribution of wealth. Our present purpose is to illustrate
the uses of the marginal conception. Our practical
economic problems would be better understood, if the
public generally were a little less disposed to think in
terms of averages, and a little more in terms of margins,
if we all of us instinctively realized that the cost that
really matters is the cost at which additional production
is profitable under the conditions ruling at the time,
or in the immediate future.

§ 6.   *General Relation between Price, Utility and Cost.*
Let us conclude this chapter by summing up the conclusions which have emerged as to the relations of
utility and cost to price.

The price of a commodity is determined by the conditions of both supply and demand; and neither can
logically be said to be the superior influence, though
it may sometimes be convenient to concentrate our
attention on one or other of them. The chief factor
on which the conditions of demand depend is the
utility (as measured in terms of money). The chief
factor on which the conditions of supply depend is the
cost of production (again as measured in terms of

money). The prevailing trend towards an equilibrium of demand and supply can thus be expressed as follows :—

VI. A commodity tends to be produced on a scale at which its marginal cost of production is equal to its marginal utility, as measured in terms of money, and both are equal to its price.

CHAPTER V

JOINT DEMAND AND SUPPLY

§ 1. *Marginal Cost under Joint Supply.* Several references have been made above to joint products, a relation which it will be convenient now to describe as that of Joint Supply. Our sense of symmetry should make us look for a parallel relation on the side of demand ; and it is not far to seek. There is a " joint demand " for carriage and horses, for golf clubs and golf balls, for pens and ink, for the many groups of things which we use together in ordinary life. But the most important instances of Joint Demand are to be found when we pass from consumers' to producers' goods. There, indeed, Joint Demand is the universal rule. Iron ore, coal and the services of many grades of operatives are all jointly demanded for the production of steel ; wool, textile machinery and again the services of many operatives are jointly demanded for the production of woollen goods (to mention in each case only a few things out of a very extensive list). Now we have already noted that, when commodities are jointly supplied. there is an obvious difficulty in allocating to each of them its proper share of the joint cost of production. There is a similar difficulty in estimating the utility of a commodity which is demanded jointly with others. Thus, the utility of wool is derived from that of the woollen goods which it helps to make. But the utility of the factories, the machinery and the operatives employed in the woollen and worsted industries is derived from precisely the same source. How much, then, of the utility of woollen goods should be attributed to the wool and how much to the textile machinery ? Can we make any sense of the notion of utility as applying to one of these things, taken by itself ? And, if not, how can we explain the price of a thing like wool in terms of utility and cost, since we cannot disentangle its cost from that of mutton, nor its utility from that of a great variety of other things ?

Here the conception of the margin enables us to grapple with a problem which would otherwise be insoluble. For, while it is impossible to separate out the total utility and cost of wool, it is not impossible to disentangle its marginal utility and its marginal cost. The proportion in which wool and mutton are supplied cannot be radically transformed ; but it can be varied within certain limits, by rearing, for instance, a different breed of sheep. Variations of this kind have been an important feature of the economic history of Australasia, where sheep farming is the leading industry. Before the days of cold storage, Australia and New Zealand could not export their mutton to European markets, though they could export their wool. Wool was accordingly much the most valuable product ; the mutton was sold in the home markets, where, the supply being very plentiful, the price was very low. In the circumstances, the Australasian farmers naturally concentrated on breeding a variety of sheep whose wool-yielding were

F

superior to their mutton-yielding qualities. The development of the arts of refrigeration led in the eighties to an important change. It became possible to obtain relatively high prices for frozen mutton in overseas markets. There was, therefore, a marked tendency, especially in New Zealand, to substitute, for the merino, the crossbred sheep which yields a larger quantity of mutton and a smaller quantity of wool of poorer quality. Now if we calculate the cost of maintaining the number of merino sheep which will yield a given quantity of wool, and calculate the cost of maintaining the larger number of crossbred sheep which will be required to yield the *same* quantity of wool (allowing for differences of quality) the extra cost which would be incurred in the latter case must be attributed entirely to the extra mutton that would be obtained. This extra cost we can regard as constituting the marginal cost of mutton. So long as this marginal cost falls short of the price of mutton, it will be profitable to extend further the substitution of crossbred for merino sheep. The process of substitution will in fact be continued until we reach the point at which the marginal cost is about equal to the price. Similarly by starting with the numbers of merino and crossbred sheep which would yield the same quantity of mutton, we can calculate the marginal cost of wool; and again the tendency will be for this marginal cost to be equal to the price.[1]

[1] It may be found difficult to grasp this point when stated in general terms. The following arithmetical example may make it plainer:—

Suppose a merino sheep yields 9 units of mutton and 10 units of wool.

Suppose a crossbred sheep yields 10 units of mutton and 8 units of wool.

§ 2. *Marginal Utility under Joint Demand.* On the side of demand there exist as a rule similar possibilities of variation. *Some* machinery, *some* labour, *some* materials of various kinds, are all indispensable in the production of any manufactured commodity. But the proportions in which these factors are combined together can be varied, and are frequently varied in practice as the result of the ceaseless pursuit of economy by business men. To produce pig-iron, you need both coal and iron ore ; but, if coal becomes more costly, it is possible to economize its use. Machinery and labour must be

Suppose, further, that a merino sheep and a crossbred sheep each cost the same sum, say, for convenience, £10, to rear and maintain ; and that there are no special costs assignable to the wool and the mutton respectively, as, of course, in fact there are.

Then 10 merino sheep, yielding 90 units of mutton+100 units of wool, cost £100 ; while 9 crossbred sheep, yielding 90 units of mutton+72 units of wool, cost £90.

Hence you could obtain an extra 28 units of wool for an extra cost of £10, by maintaining 10 merino sheep rather than 9 crossbred sheep. The marginal cost of wool is thus $£\frac{10}{28}$ per unit.

Similarly 8 merino sheep, yielding 72 units of mutton+80 units of wool, cost £80 ; while 10 crossbred sheep, yielding 100 units of mutton+80 units of wool, cost £100.

Hence you could obtain an extra 28 units of mutton for an extra cost of £20, by maintaining 10 crossbred sheep in place of 8 merinos. The marginal cost of mutton is thus $£\frac{20}{28}$ per unit.

So long as the price obtainable for wool exceeds $£\frac{10}{28}$, and that obtainable for mutton does not exceed $£\frac{20}{28}$ per unit, it will pay to substitute merino for crossbred ; and conversely. If the price of wool exceeds $£\frac{10}{28}$ and the price of mutton also exceeds $£\frac{20}{28}$, it will be profitable to expand the supply of both breeds, until, as the result of the increased supply, one of the above conditions ceases to obtain. Conversely, if the prices of both products are less than the figures indicated, sheep farming of both kinds will be restricted. The resultant of the processes of expansion or restriction, and substitution, will be that, unless one of the breeds is eliminated, the prices of mutton and wool will equal their respective marginal costs. These marginal costs may, of course, alter as the process of substitution extends. For the relative cost of maintaining merinos and crossbreds will not be the same for every farmer. Here again it is the costs at the " margin of substitution " that matter.

used together, in some cases in proportions which are absolutely fixed. But there is in nearly every industry a debated question as to whether the introduction of some further labour-saving machine would be worth while, or some improved machine which would represent the substitution of more capital plus less labour for less capital plus more labour. A farmer can cultivate his land, to use a common expression, more intensively or less jntensively ; in other words, he can apply larger or smaller quantities of capital and labour (the proportion between which he can also vary) to the same amount of land. The problem is essentially the same as that of the substitution of the crossbred for the merino. We can take the various possible combinations of the factors of production, and contrast two cases in which different quantities of one factor are employed, together with equal quantities of the others. The extra product which will be yielded in the case in which the larger quantity of the varying factor is employed can then be regarded as the marginal product (or marginal utility) of the extra quantity of that factor ; and we can say that the employment of this factor will be pushed forward to the point where this marginal product will be roughly equal to the price that must be paid for it. We can thus lay down the most important proposition that the relation between marginal utility and price holds good generally of the ultimate agents of production ; that the rent of land, the wages of labour, and, we can even add, the profits of capital tend to equal their (derived) marginal utilities, or, as it is sometimes expressed, their marginal net products.

Whenever, therefore, the proportions in which two or

more things are produced or used together can be
varied, the relations of joint supply and joint demand
are perfectly consistent with a specific marginal cost
and marginal utility for each commodity.

§ 3. *A Contrast between Cotton and Cotton-seed, and
Wool and Mutton.* But it sometimes happens that such
variations cannot be made. Thus, it has not been
found possible (so far as I am aware) to alter the
proportions in which cotton lint and cotton-seed are
yielded by the cotton plant. Roughly speaking, you
get about 2 lb. of cotton-seed for every 1 lb. of cotton
lint (or raw cotton), and though this proportion may
vary somewhat from plantation to plantation, it is
upon the knees of the gods, and not upon the will of the
planter that the variation depends. We cannot, therefore, speak with accuracy of the separate marginal costs
of raw cotton and cotton-seed. It is true that some
plantations are so far distant from any seed-crushing
mill that it is not worth while to sell the seed as a
commercial product ; and it might seem, therefore,
as though we could regard the entire costs of cotton
growing on *such* plantations as constituting the marginal
costs of raw cotton. But planters, so situated, derive a
considerable value from their cotton-seed by using it as
fodder for their live stock or as a manure. You can,
of course, argue that proper allowance is automatically
made for this factor, as a deduction from the costs of
raw cotton, when you add up the expenses of the
plantation. In the same way you can deduct the price
which a planter who sells his cotton-seed obtains for it,
from the total costs of the plantation, and call the

remainder the costs of the raw cotton. But this is really to reason in a circle. For in either case the magnitude of the deduction depends on the marginal utility of the cotton-seed. And the notion of the cost of anything becomes blurred and blunted if we so use it that it must be deduced from the utility of something else, which is not an agent in the production of the thing in question.

This point is not merely an academic one. It means that we cannot explain the *relative* prices of cotton lint and cotton-seed in terms of cost at all, whether marginal or otherwise. The influence of cost will be confined to the *sum* of the prices of the two things. Upon this sum it will exert precisely the same influence as it exerts upon price in general, by affecting the total quantities of the two things that will be supplied. But upon the distribution of this sum between lint and seed, cost will exert no influence whatever, because it cannot affect the proportions in which they are supplied. It may assist some readers if I state the matter in more concrete terms. Cost of production will be one of the factors which will result in the production of an annual cotton crop in the United States of, let us say, 10 million tons of seed cotton. This crop will yield roughly $6\frac{2}{3}$ million tons of cotton-seed, and $3\frac{1}{3}$ million tons (or rather more than 13 million bales) of lint. The combined price received by the planter of (let us say) 14·4 cents for 1 lb. of lint plus 2 lb. of seed should correspond roughly to the marginal joint costs of production. But the factor of cost has no influence at all in determining that this combined price is made up of a price of 12 cents per lb. for lint, and only 1·2 cents per lb. (or $24 per ton) for cotton-seed. To account for this we must rely entirely upon demand. We can say, shortly, that the respective prices must be such as will enable the demand to carry off $6\frac{2}{3}$ million tons of seed. and $3\frac{1}{3}$ million tons of raw cotton. Or we can go further and say that the marginal utility of a pound of raw cotton, when $3\frac{1}{3}$ million tons are supplied, is ten times as great as that of a pound of seed when $6\frac{2}{3}$ million tons are supplied.

If accordingly the demand for cotton-seed were to expand considerably owing, say, to the discovery of some new use for the oil, which is its most valuable constituent ; the effect would be first a rise in the price of cotton-seed, and, subsequently, by stimulating cotton growing, a more plentiful supply and a lower price for raw cotton. And so far at least as the increased supply is concerned, this must necessarily be the effect, " other things being equal " ; though, to be sure, it might be outweighed and obscured by other influences such as the boll-weevil. But it is *not* the case that an increased demand for mutton must necessarily increase the supply or lower the price of wool ; and it is most unlikely to do so in any similar degree. For, here, the separate marginal costs of the two things exert their influence. An increased demand for mutton will stimulate sheep farming, but it will also stimulate the substitution of crossbred for merino breeds ; and the resultant of these two opposite tendencies upon the supply of wool is logically indeterminate. As a matter of history we know that the development of cold storage in the eighties (which we may regard for the present purpose as equivalent to an increased demand for Australian mutton)

caused considerable perturbation in the woollen and
worsted industries of Yorkshire. They were faced with
a dwindling supply and a soaring price of merino wool ;
and the adaptability with which they met the situation,
and won prestige for the crossbred tops, and yarns
and fabrics, to which they largely turned is a matter of
just pride in the trade to-day. The fact, however, that
this alteration in the supply of wool was a matter
not only of quantity but of quality, while it takes
nothing from the substance of the preceding argument,
makes it difficult to draw a clear moral, bearing on the
present issue, from this incursion into history.

§ 4. *The Importance of being Unimportant.* The above
contrast between cases in which variation is possible,
and those in which it is not possible, is reproduced with
a heightened significance when we turn back to joint
demand. The cases are perhaps less common in which
it is *impossible* to alter the proportions in which different
commodities are jointly demanded, but there are many
cases in which it is not nearly worth while to do so
(and this amounts to very much the same thing).
Cases of this sort are especially likely to occur when we
are dealing with a commodity which accounts for only
a tiny fraction of the costs of the industry which is its
chief consumer. Sewing cotton, for example, is jointly
demanded, with many other things, by the tailoring
and other clothing trades ; but the money which these
trades spend on sewing cotton is so small a part of their
total expenditure, that no ordinary variation in
its price is likely to make it worth while to study the
ways and means of using it in smaller quantities. When

sewing cotton is bought by the domestic consumer, considerations which are fundamentally the same, though somewhat different in form, point to a similar conclusion. It is thus very difficult to assign to sewing cotton a specific marginal utility. This difficulty is of great importance in connection with the possibilities of monopolistic exploitation. For it means that the demand blade of the scissors upon which we rely to cut off excrescences of price is blunted, and if accordingly the producers constitute a strong enough combination to control the supply blade, they will possess an unusual power of advancing their selling prices as they choose. I am far from suggesting that Messrs. J. & P. Coats are to be condemned as an extortionate monopoly. On the contrary, during 1919, when the profits in highly competitive industries like the main branches of the cotton and woollen trades, soared exuberantly, the record of this concern seems to me one of distinct moderation. But the present point is that they possess an exceptional *power* to fix the price of sewing cotton as they choose, and that this is attributable in no small degree to the fact that sewing cotton constitutes an essential but relatively trifling item in the expenses of the processes in which it is employed.

Perhaps the point will be made clearer if we turn from the selling prices of commercial products, in regard to which there is a strong and not ineffective public sentiment against " profiteering," to the remuneration of different classes of labour. With an instinctive disposition towards megalomania, we often speak in Great Britain as though the miners, being a very numerous and well-organized body of workpeople, were in a stronger strategic position than most work-people for exacting the remuneration they desire. It is quite true that a stoppage of work in the coal industry causes us a high degree of inconvenience, and temporary concessions may thereby be obtained which might otherwise have been refused. But this is a dubious advantage, and we grossly exaggerate its real importance. The truth is that the strategic position of the miners in regard to wages questions is by no means strong. For their wages constitute a very large percentage of the cost of coal ; and the price of coal in its turn is a most important element in the costs of many of the industries which are its principal consumers. Great Britain, moreover, is far from possessing a monopoly of coal. If, accordingly, the wages of the miners are temporarily pushed up to a high point, the result will certainly be a diminished demand for British coal, which will lead before long to their fighting a losing battle to maintain the concessions they have won. Contrast their position with that of the steel smelters, whose wages constitute a very small percentage of the costs of steel production, and we must agree I think that we have in this distinction the main reason why the steel smelters, though they hardly ever go on strike, have as a rule been able to do so much better for themselves than have the miners.

When a commodity or service is such that an appreci-able alteration in its price has only a slight effect upon the quantity demanded, the demand is said to be *inelastic*. Conversely, when a small change in price greatly alters the quantity demanded, we call the demand *elastic*. In the former case, it is worth noting, a larger aggregate sum of money will be spent upon the thing when its price is high than when it is low, while the opposite is true in the latter case. This distinction is of considerable importance in connection with many problems (e.g. of taxation); and the terms, elastic demand and inelastic demand, are worth remembering. We may thus express the above conclusions by saying that the demand for sewing-cotton is highly inelastic, and that the demand for coal miners is more elastic than that for steel smelters.

§ 5. *Capital and Labour.* Cases in which it is impracticable to make any variation in the proportions in which different things are used together are, however, the exception rather than the rule. Where variation is possible, we are confronted with an uncertainty as to the way in which an increased supply of one thing will react on the demand for another, similiar to our uncertainty as to whether an increased demand for mutton would augment or diminish the supply of wool. It is, for instance, of the highest importance to give a clear answer, if we can, to the question whether an increased supply of capital will increase the demand for labour. The chief effect of an increased supply of capital is to facilitate the extended use of expensive machines : to some extent these machines will increase the demand for labour ; to some extent they will be substituted for it. Which of these two tendencies will outweigh the other we cannot be absolutely sure. But fortunately we can be far more nearly sure than was possible in the analogous case of wool and mutton. An increase in the supply of capital increases the demand for the commodities, from which the demand for labour is derived, in both the senses discussed in Chapter II. First it makes them cheaper to buy, and thus increases the quantity that will be bought. It is this that is parallel to the effect of an increased demand for mutton in making it more profitable to breed sheep. But it also serves to increase the purchasing power with which to buy commodities, because it increases the aggregate real wealth of the community, and it thus serves to raise the whole demand curve. This last consideration is so important as to make it overwhelmingly probable, apart from the evidence of history, that an increase in the supply of capital (and the same may be said of an increase in the supply of the other agents of production) will on balance increase the demand for labour. The evidence of history points to the same conclusion. The history of the last hundred years displays an unprecedented accumulation of capital, and an unprecedented extension of machinery, associated with an unprecedented improvement in the standard of living throughout the whole community. This is powerful testimony in favour of the view that an increase in the supply of capital and the use of machinery will usually enhance on balance the demand for labour. Moreover, though this is not conclusive, there is little room for doubt that an obstructive attitude towards the extension of machinery in a particular country, or a particular district, is misguided. For its effect must be to make production more costly there than it is elsewhere, and to lead, slowly perhaps, but very surely, to the transference of the industry to other regions.

§ 6. *Conclusions as to Joint Supply and Joint Demand.*

Here, however, we are beginning to digress. Let us sum up in a general form our conclusions as to the way in which changes in the supply or demand of a commodity react upon the demand or supply of the other things with which it is jointly demanded or supplied. Everything turns, as we have seen, on the possibility of variation in the proportions in which the things are used or produced together; and this, it is also clear, is a matter of degree. Our conclusions, therefore, had best take the following form :—

VII. When two or more things are jointly demanded, in proportions which cannot easily be varied, the tendency will be for an increase (or decrease) in the supply of one of them to increase (or decrease) the demand for the others. These results will be more certain, and more marked, the more difficult it is to vary the proportions in which the things are used.

Similarly, when two or more things are jointly supplied, in proportions which cannot easily be varied, the tendency will be for an increase (or decrease) in the demand for one of them to increase (or decrease) the supply of the others. These results again will be more certain and more marked, the more difficult it is to vary the proportions in which the things are supplied.

§ 7. *Composite Supply and Composite Demand.* Joint Demand and Joint Supply do not complete the list of relations between the demand and supply of different things. Between tea and coffee, or beef and mutton there is a relation of a different kind. These things are in large measure what we call "substitutes" for one another. An increased supply, and a lower price of mutton, will probably induce us to consume less beef. This relation it is convenient to describe as Composite Supply. Beef and mutton make up a composite supply of meat ; tea and coffee a composite supply of a certain type of beverage. For any group of things, between which the relation of Composite Supply exists, we can say, with complete generality, that an increased supply of one of them will tend to diminish the demand for the others. Parallel to the relation of Composite Supply is that of Composite Demand. There are frequently several alternative uses in which a commodity or service can be employed ; and these alternative uses make up a composite demand for the thing in question. Thus railways, gasworks, private households and a great variety of industries contribute to a Composite Demand for coal. It is worth noting that there is frequently an association in practice between Joint Demand and Composite Supply on the one hand ; and between Joint Supply and Composite Demand on the other. Wool and mutton, for instance, we have described as an instance of Joint Supply ; but, in so far as the proportions of wool and mutton can be varied, we can regard these things as constituting a Composite Demand for sheep. And this conception may help us to retain a clearer and more orderly picture of the problems we have discussed above. We can regard the fact that wool and mutton are produced together as their Joint Supply aspect, and the fact that these proportions can be varied as their Composite Demand aspect ; and the question as to whether an increased demand for mutton will increase the supply of wool turns upon whether the former aspect is more important than the latter. Similarly labour and machinery, employed together for the same purpose, form an instance of Joint Demand ; but in so far as they can be substituted for one another, they constitute a Composite Supply of alternative agents of production.

These four relations of Joint Demand, Joint Supply, Composite Demand and Composite Supply are well worth remembering and distinguishing from one another. They are of immense importance in every branch of economic affairs. There are hardly any economic problems upon which we are fitted to express an opinion, unless we have a lively sense of the far-reaching ramifications of cause and consequence, of the subtle and often unexpected interconnections between different industries and different markets. To gape at these complexities in a confused stupor is as foolish as it is to ignore them. But confusion and stupor are only too likely to represent our final state of mind, if we attempt to deal with these complications, one by one as they occur to us, in a piecemeal and haphazard fashion. We need a clear method, a systematic plan by which we may search them out, and fit them into place. The four relations which we have enumerated supply us with such a plan and method. For they represent something more than a series of pompous names for familiar notions. They constitute a classification of the various ways in which the demand and supply of one thing can affect the demand and supply of others ; a classification which is exhaustive when we add the relation of derived demand, and an analogous relation on the supply side which we must now notice.

§ 8. *Ultimate Real Costs.* Just as the utility of " producers' goods " is derived from that of the " consumers' goods " which they help to make ; so the cost of any commodity is derived from the cost of the things which help to make it. Moreover, just as we recognize that the utility of " consumers' goods " lies at the back of all demand, and constitutes the ultimate end of all production ; so we cannot but feel, however obscurely, that behind the phenomena of money costs, there must lie certain ultimate costs, of which all money costs are but the measure. But when we try to explain what the nature of these real costs may be, we are plunged in difficulty. Wages, it may indeed seem at first sight, present no trouble. There is the effort and the fatigue, the unpleasantness of human labour, to represent real costs. But can we suppose that these things are measured with any approach to accuracy by the wages which are paid in actual fact ? Is it true, even as a broad general rule, that the services which are most arduous and most disagreeable command the highest price ? And wages are not the only ingredient of money costs. There are profits : to what real costs do profits correspond ? More difficult conundrum still, to what does rent ? These plainly are not questions upon which he who runs may read. It will be necessary to devote the next four chapters to their elucidation.

CHAPTER VI

LAND

§ 1. *The Special Characteristics of Land*. In the great process of co-operation by which the wants of mankind are supplied, Nature is an indispensable participant. She renders her assistance in an infinite variety of ways, of which the properties of the soil which man cultivates form only one ; but the sunshine and rain which enable the farmer to grow his crops ; the coal and iron ore beneath the surface of the earth, can be regarded for our present purpose as forming part of the land with which they are associated. We can thus concentrate upon land as the representative of the free gifts of nature, which are of economic significance. Land in modern communities is for the most part privately owned. It can be bought and sold for a price, and acquired by inheritance. Moreover, it is a common practice, particularly in the United Kingdom, for an owner who does not wish himself to cultivate or otherwise use the land, not to sell it to the man who does, but to lease it to him for a term of years for an annual payment which we term rent. It is therefore natural and convenient to envisage the problems, which we shall consider in this chapter, as problems concerning the price and rent of land. But, once again,

G

the laws and principles which we shall state and illustrate in terms of the current systems of ownership and tenure, possess a much deeper significance than this terminology might suggest.

The fact that Land is a free gift of nature distinguishes it in various ways from commodities which are produced by man. The peculiarities which are most important from the economic standpoint are (1) that the supply of land is, broadly speaking, fixed and unalterable, and (2) that its quality and value vary, from piece to piece, with a variation which is immense in its range, but fairly continuous in its gradation. These are thus two aspects from which the phenomena of price and rent can be regarded; aspects which it is usual to call, (1) the scarcity aspect, (2) the differential aspect.

§ 2. *The Scarcity Aspect.* The fact that the supply of land is fixed has the following significance. If the demand for land increases, the price will tend to rise. This is also true, for a short period at least, of an ordinary commodity. But, in the latter case, there would ensue an increase in supply which would serve to check the rise in price, and possibly, if production on a larger scale led to improved methods of production, bring the price down eventually below its original level. In the case of land, no such reaction is possible. There is nothing, therefore, to restrain the price (and the rent) of land from rising indefinitely, and without limit, if the demand for it should continue to increase. Conversely, if the demand for land falls off, there is nothing to check the consequent fall in price and rent. In the case of ordinary commodities, the supply would be diminished, because most things are either consumed by being used, or wear out in the course of time, and a regular annual production is therefore necessary to sustain their supply at the existing level. But land remains, whether it is used or not ; and its supply is, broadly speaking, just as incapable of being diminished, as it is of being increased. Changes in the demand for land in either direction are thus likely to affect its price in a much greater degree than that in which the price of an ordinary commodity will be affected by a corresponding change in its demand.

For most purposes, however, it is of more interest to compare land with other agents of production, especially with capital and labour, rather than with ordinary commodities. Now, as we have already noted, there is some doubt as to the manner in which the supply of capital or labour is likely to be affected by alterations in demand price. But the supply of capital and the supply of labour, even if we suppose them to be as entirely unresponsive to price changes as is the supply of land, are at any rate not fixed. Not only *may* they vary for many reasons, but they are in fact likely to vary in direct proportion to the population. An increase in population implies an increase in the supply of labour ; and it is likely to be accompanied by an increase in the supply of capital ; in other words, the supply of these agents will expand, as the demand for them expands. But the supply of land will remain what it was. This fact is enormously important in connection with the broad problem of population, which will form the theme of another volume.

But it is important also in other connections. It has been the dominating factor in many absorbing controversies upon high policy regarding the ownership of land, or the taxation of land values, upon which we can touch but lightly here. It has seemed to many writers a reasonable proposition to lay down, that the ordinary course of the progress of society, the increase of population and industry, must mean, as a broad general rule, a constant increase in the demand for land. And, if that be granted, it seems to follow that the price and rent of land will tend constantly to increase. John Stuart Mill, accordingly, in the middle of the last century, asserted that "the ordinary progress of a society, which increases in wealth, is at all times tending to augment the incomes of landlords; to give them both a greater amount and a greater proportion of the wealth of the community, independently of any trouble or outlay, incurred by themselves,"[1] and upon the strength of this assertion, he justified the policy of imposing a special tax upon what we have come to call the "unearned increment" of land. But how far does actual experience bear his assertion out? In Great Britain we have seen in the last half-century an undoubted increase in urban rents; but over long periods at least, there was a marked fall in both the prices and rents of agricultural land, despite the fact that the country was "increasing in wealth" as rapidly as ever before. This was due, of course, in the main to the increased supplies of wheat and other foodstuffs coming from the New World: and if, accordingly, we choose to lump together not only our own

[1] *Principles of Political Economy*, by John Stuart Mill.

urban and agricultural land, but the land of other
countries as well, and to speak vaguely of the demand
for land as a whole, it might seem as though we could
argue that Mill's generalization still holds good. But
even this is by no means certain and in any case such a
generalization is of very little service : what the
illustration should rather suggest to us, is the danger
of speaking of land vaguely as a whole, and the importance of turning our attention to the variations in value
between different kinds and different pieces.

§ 3. *The Differential Aspect.* Most ordinary commodities
are not produced on a single, uniform pattern. As a
rule there are many variations of grade and quality,
and consequently of price. But these variations are
usually designed to meet the differences of taste among
the purchasers, and we do not expect to find that any
variety of an ordinary commodity will be produced,
which is so poor in quality as to be entirely valueless.
But since it is nature which has produced the land,
without any assistance or guidance from man, there are
many pieces of land which are so unfertile, or are otherwise so unsuitable for productive purposes, as to be
quite valueless from the economic standpoint. Even
in a densely populated country like Great Britain, there
are considerable tracts of land which it is unprofitable
to employ for any economic purpose whatsoever, and
which possess no further value than what the mere
pride of ownership may give them. This fact makes it
possible to apply the conception of the margin to the
case of Land with particularly illuminating results.

In the first place, however, it should be observed

that the value of any piece of land does not depend
solely on the intrinsic fertility of the soil. The fact that
land is an immobile thing makes its *situation* a factor of
great importance. In the case of urban land, situation
is, of course, the only thing that counts. The value of
a site in Bond Street or the City is entirely unaffected
by its capacity or incapacity for potato-growing
purposes. But even for agricultural land, situation is a
most important matter. A farm, which is so remote
that considerable transport charges must be incurred
to bring its produce to market, will be less sought after,
and less valuable, than one which is much better
situated though somewhat less fertile. In what follows,
therefore, we must speak of the " quality " of a piece
of land in a broad sense to include advantages of
situation, as well as of fertility. Let us now, imagine
the different pieces of land in Great Britain to be
arranged in order of quality, so that we have a long
series, with land of the best quality at one end, and of
the poorest quality at the other. At the latter end, we
will have such land as is found near the top of Snowdon
or Ben Nevis, which it clearly does not pay to cultivate
at all. Somewhere, then, between these two extremes,
we shall come to a point where the land is just, but only
just, worth cultivating, or where, to revert to a form
of words we previously employed, it is a matter of *doubt*,
whether the land is really worth using for a productive
purpose. Such land we can regard as the " marginal
land " ; and since the variety of nature is at once
infinite and fairly minutely graduated we shall probably
find that on one side of this margin there is much land
which is only slightly superior, and on the other, much

which is only slightly inferior, to the marginal land itself. What, then, is likely to be the value and the rent of this marginal land, this land which is just on the " margin of cultivation " ? Some readers may find the answer startling. The rent of the marginal land will be nil, because it will not pay to cultivate it, if any appreciable rent is charged. A piece of land for which it is worth a tenant's while to pay an appreciable rent, will not be the marginal land, because there will be land just slightly inferior to it which it will also pay to cultivate if a somewhat lower rent is charged. And so we can pass to poorer and poorer qualities of land, with an ever diminishing rent, until at the margin of cultivation the derived utility of the land is negligible and the rent vanishes.

This certainly is a somewhat abstract conception ; but it is by no means so remote from reality as may at first sight appear. The reader may protest that in the course of an extensive and varied acquaintance with landowners, he has not yet run across this peculiar marginal type, who lets his land for no rent at all. But there, if his experience is really extensive, I think he is mistaken. It so happens that the ordinary agricultural landowner leases out his land, not by itself, but together with a variety of other things such as farm buildings, which it costs him a considerable sum of money to provide. He will not as a rule be willing to go to this expense, unless he sees his way to obtain for the farm an annual payment, which represents at least a fair return on this capital outlay, as big a return as he could have got, for instance, by investing the same amount of money in some gilt-edged security. This annual payment will, it is true, be called rent; but the significance of this is that what we term rent in ordinary life is usually a complex thing, made up of two essentially distinct elements, viz. the normal return on the capital goods supplied together with the land, and what we may call the " net rent," or the " pure rent " attributable to the land itself. Now will any reader make so bold as to say that there is no land under cultivation, in respect of which this net rent is either nil or negligible ? The landowners will not agree with him. It is not a question, it should be observed, as to whether the rent obtained represents more than a fair return on the purchase price paid for the land ; that is quite another matter. The question is whether the rent obtained exceeds a fair return on the capital sum spent on the buildings, etc. ; with which every farm must be equipped to let at all. In fact there are not a few farms in Great Britain where there is no such excess, and where accordingly there is no " net rent " or " pure rent " which can be attributed to the land.

The question whether it would be profitable to cultivate any piece of land, turns upon whether the receipts which would be obtained by selling the produce would exceed the costs of cultivation : and under these costs of cultivation we must include, of course, the remuneration of the farmer's services. Farmers, like other people, have to live ; and they would not take on the troublesome job of farming, unless there seemed a prospect of making a living out of it. The remuneration of the farmer takes, of course, the form not of a salary, but of profits : and these profits vary very much from year to year, and from place to place, and from man to man. They must cover not only the remuneration of the farmer's services, but interest on his capital, and a payment for the considerable risk he undertakes. Thus it will not be worth while to cultivate a piece of land, and the land will in fact lie unused, upon which a careful farmer might obtain a profit in the ordinary sense, of no more than £10 or £20 a year. The marginal land will be land which yields a decent profit to a decent farmer, as well as a gross rent to the landowner, sufficient to compensate him for his capital outlay, but nothing further.

What, then, will be the rent of a fertile and well-situated farm, about which there is no doubt that it is well worth cultivating ? Part of the gross rent which the landowner receives must again be regarded as merely a return for the capital expended in equipping the farm for use ; but in this case, there will be a residue left over, which constitutes the net rent of the land. The net rent will measure the derived utility of the land to its occupier, and will in general represent (very roughly, of course, in practice) the differential advantage of cultivating the land in question rather than land on the " margin of cultivation." This differential advantage may take either, or both, of the forms, of a larger produce per acre, or a lower cost of production and marketing. But, in any case, the extra profit, which, if no rent were charged, a decent farmer could obtain by cultivating the farm in question, rather than a marginal farm, will be roughly equal to the net rent which his landlord can exact from him, if his landlord so chooses. The landlord may, of course, not choose to exact a rent so high as this ; and as a matter of fact, in a country like

Great Britain landlords often content themselves with less. The traditions associated with the ownership of agricultural land, and with the relations between landlord and tenant serve to soften the edge of economic law, and to subject the rents which are actually fixed to the control in no small measure of the general sense of what is fair or customary. In such cases the landlord makes the farmer a present, for the time being, of part of the economic rent. On the other hand, as Irish agrarian history well illustrates, the landlord may sometimes expropriate under the name of rent, permanent improvements which are due to the labours or the expenditure of the tenant. This is, of course, particularly likely to happen, whenever it is the custom to leave to the tenant the obligation of providing the capital equipment of the farm, which in Great Britain is, for the most part, the recognized duty of the owner. Again, in the case of urban land in the South of England, expropriations of this kind are an essential and well-understood feature of the leasehold system. The owner grants a lease for a long period of time, usually ninety-nine years, for a ground rent, which is notoriously below the true economic rent of the land, subject to the condition that the leaseholder must erect upon the land and keep in good repair certain buildings, which on expiry of the lease will become the property of the ground owner. Here the nominal ground rent is only part of the total rent which is really paid ; the ultimate transference of the buildings representing often the more important part. There is, in fact, a great variety of systems of land tenure, some of which are highly complex, the respective merits of which vary greatly, and which constitute a most important problem for statesmen and legislators. Considerations of this kind in no way diminish the importance of the general analysis of rent, which we are pursuing in the present chapter. Rather they make it the more important, because we cannot properly weigh the merits of any system of land tenure, until we have grasped clearly the principles governing the rent of land in the purest form. But certainly we must never forget that the rent we are discussing may differ very greatly from, though it will vitally influence, the money payments which are called rent in actual life. It is the pure economic rent, the rent which represents the *full* annual payment which it would be worth paying to obtain the use of the land alone, which will measure, as we have said, the differential advantage of the land in question over land on the margin of cultivation.

A clear grasp of this relation helps us to perceive that an increase in the prosperity of the community may sometimes influence rents in an unexpected way. It all depends on the causes which have given rise to the increased prosperity. An advance, for instance, in agricultural science will facilitate a more abundant supply of foodstuffs ; but it will not necessarily increase the aggregate rents of agricultural land. For if it takes the form, say, of the discovery of some new artificial manure, it will very likely facilitate production on the less fertile soils far more than it will on the more fertile soils where artificial manures are not so necessary. It will thus tend to diminish the differential advantages of working on the more fertile farms, and their rents will accordingly fall, possibly by much more in the aggregate than any increase in the rents of the farms near the margin of cultivation. The point may, perhaps, be better understood if we pass from agricultural to urban land, and ask what would be the effect on site values of a great improvement in the facilities of internal transport. Push the case to an extreme, and suppose passenger transport to become so cheap and so quick that there ceases to be any advantage in living in a town so as to be near your place of work. Urban landlords would no longer be able to obtain the high rents they now receive for the sites of houses in or near a town. For most people would prefer to move out into the country where sites can be obtained at little more than an agricultural rent. The country covers so large an area relatively to the towns that the supply of rural sites would be still very plentiful as compared with the demand. Their rents would not, therefore, rise by very much, although the rents of the housing sites in towns would fall heavily. Of course, there are other factors to be taken into account before we could pronounce upon the effect on aggregate rents. Central sites for shops might, for instance, fetch a higher rental than before. The purpose of this discussion is not to generalize, but to show the danger of generalizing about rents in the aggregate, or land as a whole.

§ 4. *The Margin of Transference.* The last illustration may serve, however, to remind us of an obvious fact which we must now take into account. The same piece of land may be used for a variety of purposes. It may have been used for growing corn, and later it may be devoted to the building of houses, or, as at Slough, to a repair depôt for motor vehicles. It need hardly be said that the land will, as a general rule, be put to the use in which its value is greatest ; or to speak more strictly, in which the biggest rent, or the biggest selling price can be obtained. But the notion of the differential advantages which a piece of land possesses over the marginal land becomes decidedly more complicated when we take account of this variety of uses. Let us turn our attention, for instance, to the sites used for shop and office purposes, and consider what we can regard as the marginal site in this connection. Clearly it will not be the marginal land of which we spoke above, which it only just paid to cultivate, and which yielded no rent at all. For this will probably be agricultural land in an out-of-the-way district, where no one would dream of setting up an office or a shop. Any site upon which a sane man would contemplate setting up a shop will certainly possess value for other purposes, such as house-building. Hence the marginal site for shop-keeping purposes will not be like our marginal farm, a site which yields no rent.

As regards many pieces of land, there is no doubt as to the purposes for which they can most profitably be used. This piece will command a much higher rent as a shop site than in any other capacity ; for that piece house-building is the obvious employment ; for another, agriculture. But in quite a number of instances there is considerable uncertainty. It is not clear whether upon this site it will be better to erect a house or a shop, or if the latter, what kind of a shop. It is not clear whether it will pay to use that farm land for a building scheme ; and, within the domain of agriculture, which of course comprises an immense variety of really different industries, it is often a very moot point indeed whether a certain field should be left under grass, or brought under the plough. Cases of this sort are not phantoms of the imagination; they emerge on every side as concrete problems with which some one or other is dealing every day, and it is these cases which constitute the marginal land for the purposes of a particular occupation. The marginal sites for shops are the sites for which it is only just worth while to pay rents sufficient to entice them away from houses. And the rent for a site in Bond Street, or elsewhere, which is so much more suitable for shop purposes that no alternative use would be worth considering, will exceed the rent paid for one of these marginal sites by, roughly speaking, the extra advantage it possesses for shop purposes. Or will fall short of it, it may be well to add, to the extent of its comparative disadvantage. For there may be many such marginal sites, some of which will fetch low rents, and others very high rents indeed; the same site being often of great potential utility for a large variety of occupations. Between any two occupations there will thus usually be a *margin of transference*, which we must conceive not as a point, but as an irregular line, upon or near to which there will be many pieces of land, differing greatly in the rents which they fetch. These variations of rent will correspond to the differences between the advantages or derived utilities which the sites possess for *both* the occupations in question. The position of such margins of transference will of course alter as industrial conditions change, and, when they alter, the rents of sites which are not near any margin of transference will be affected also. Thus an increased demand for the products of any particular industry will make it profitable for that industry to offer higher rents, and thus draw land away from other occupations. This will have the effect of raising, though possibly to a very slight extent, the rents of sites which still remain in other uses ; for there will be fewer of them available ; and their derived utilities will consequently be increased.

But here, as everywhere, it is upon the margin that our attention should be focussed, because it is round about the margin (wherever it is found) that the changes are taking place which really matter for society. When Mr. Mallaby-Deeley buys an estate in Covent Garden from the Duke of Bedford, the transaction hardly deserves the degree of public interest it excites. Nothing has happened which is of material consequence to anyone except the two gentlemen concerned ; the various sites are still used for the various purposes for which they were used before ; nothing has occurred that really matters. But when houses are pulled down for the erection of a cinema, or when a field is diverted from tillage to pasture, something has happened which affects for good or ill the interests of the whole community. Conversion from tillage to pasture represents, indeed, a tendency which has been very marked in Great Britain during the last generation, and has aroused misgivings in many public-spirited observers. Possibly for a variety of reasons, these misgivings may be justified; certainly the problem is well worthy of attention. But when in this way the issue is raised of tillage versus pasture, it is essential, if we are to discuss it rationally, that we should envisage it clearly as applying only to a limited portion of agricultural land, to the portion which lies somewhere near the margin of transference, as things are now, between the two forms of agriculture. It might be socially desirable to bring under the plough a field which the farmer finds it only *slightly* more profitable to lease under grass; but this would be highly improbable in the case of a field where the balance of argument to the farmer in favour of pasture is overwhelming. The position of the margin of transference between different uses may, in other words, be somewhat out of place from the social point of view, and it may be desirable by appeals and propaganda, even conceivably by the devices of State subsidy and compulsion, to push it forwards or backwards in greater or less degree. But it will be necessarily a matter of degree, and nothing could be more foolish than to speak as though there was, or could be, some ideal method of cultivation equally applicable to all lands, without regard to their climatic and other conditions. Needless to say, none of the agricultural experts who sometimes deplore the decline of arable farming are guilty of such foolishness. But the sense of the diversity of nature which is very vivid to them may sometimes be lacking in people who live in towns, and a firm grasp of the marginal notion may serve best to keep the latter from forgetting it.

§ 5. *The Necessity of Rent.* Behind all such detailed applications there lies a more general consideration which deserves attention. The way in which the land of a country is used, the way in which it is apportioned between the countless alternative employments that are possible, is a most important matter, more important perhaps than any questions as to the size of the incomes which particular landowners receive by virtue of their rights of ownership. How is this apportionment effected as things are now ? The answer is clear : mainly by the agency of either rent or price. The business which finds it worth while to offer the highest rent or the highest price for any piece of land will, as a rule, be able to command its use. And, with this as the governing principle, an apportionment is secured between shops, offices, factories, agriculture, between the immense variety of different employments covered by each of these broad headings ; not a rigid unvarying apportionment, but one which constantly changes as economic circumstances change, and as the margin of transference between different occupations moves hither and thither. This apportionment takes place at present as the result of the independent decisions and bargains of many private individuals, who are thinking mainly of their own interests, and not of those of the community. But this state of affairs might be altered. The land might be nationalized and allocated to its various uses by the co-ordinated labours of a great State department, or some other agency of the collective will. However improbable such a change, it is perfectly conceivable. But what is not conceivable is that any State department should handle the job with a success even approaching that of the present system, unless it continued to use, as its main instrument, the criterion of either rent or price. That a piece of land would yield a higher rent in one occupation than in any other is not conclusive

H

evidence that it is best to devote it to the former purpose, but it is very good evidence, and it should be allowed to prevail unless it is demonstrably outweighed, as it possibly might often be, by considerations of a different kind. That it would not be well for the community to employ land in the city of London for corn-growing purposes, however desirable might be a revival of home agriculture, is so obvious that it may seem to have no bearing on the present issue. But it is only an extreme indication of the absurd and wasteful use of our natural resources, which would grow up slowly but surely, if we dispensed with ideas of rent and price as sordid irrelevancies, and allocated our land on the basis of a balancing of the loftiest arguments of a vague and sentimental character. If you are prepared for the distribution of land to become stereotyped, for each piece to continue indefinitely in its present use, then indeed you might dispense with rent, as primitive societies very largely do. That would mean stagnation and, for an industrial country, decay. But if changes are ever to be contemplated, a simple quantitative measure is the only safeguard against utter chaos. Thus rent, like interest, will be found indispensable as a measure under any efficient system of society, even if it might not always represent the payment of sums of money to private individuals. And that is why the principles governing rent possess, as I indicated at the outset of this chapter, an importance more fundamental than our present system of ownership and tenure.

§ 6. *The Question of Real Costs.* But we must not

forget the preliminary question that started us upon
our analysis of the agents of production. The rent
which a manufacturer or farmer has to pay for his land
he naturally includes in his cost of production. But
does this money cost to the individual correspond
to, and measure, any real cost to the community as a
whole? Here let us note in the first place that if only
we could disregard the variety of uses to which land is
put, if we could suppose that all industry was agriculture,
and that agriculture was a single industry with a single
product, we could argue that rent does not enter into
marginal costs at all. For we could regard the marginal
producer as the one working on a marginal farm,
where as we have seen there is no pure rent. The rent
which other producers have to pay would thus represent
merely the destination of the surplus profits which arise
wherever actual costs fall short of marginal costs. This
way of looking at the matter has proved attractive to
some thinkers, not in the least because of a desire to
palliate the effects of landlordism, but because it fits
in so well with our general sense of rent as a " surplus,"
and a surplus as something distinct from a necessary
price. But it is clearly illegitimate in an economic
theory which professes " to describe the facts." The
marginal land for many purposes fetches, as we have seen,
a considerable rent; and this rent is certainly part of
the marginal costs and of the necessary price of the
products of the particular industry. The answer to our
question is, however, not now very difficult to see.
Land, greatly as it differs in many respects from the
other agents of production, resembles them in the very
important respect that, being used for one purpose,

it is not available for other purposes, and that the
productive powers of the community in other directions
are thereby diminished.   This is the real cost to the
community, which attaches to the products of any
industry, in virtue of the land which it occupies;
not any human labours or sacrifices required to
produce the land itself, but the curtailment of the
natural resources available for productive use elsewhere.
This is the real cost of which rent is the money measure,
and generally speaking an accurate measure at the
margin of transference between one occupation and
another.   A somewhat fanciful use of the term cost,
this may seem perhaps, one not quite in accordance
with our instinctive sense of what real costs should be.
But possibly the real costs represented by wages and
profits may turn out to be not so very different, and
we had best leave the matter there, until we have
examined the nature of these other costs.

§ 7.   *Rent and Selling Price.*   In this chapter we have
spoken mainly of the rent rather than the price of land :
the relation between the two things is fairly obvious
and well understood, but it will be well not to close
the chapter without a brief account of it.   The price of
any piece of land is affected by all the considerations on
which its rent depends, but it is also affected by another
factor which has no influence whatever upon rent.
This factor is the rate of interest.   The higher the rate
of interest, the higher the return which a man could
obtain by buying gilt-edged securities, the lower will
be the price that he will pay for a piece of land which
yields a given rent.   We can express the relation more

precisely by the formula Price $=\dfrac{\text{Rent} \times 100}{\text{Rate of Interest}}$, though we must be careful, in applying this formula in practice to allow for the possible deviations between the nominal and the true rent, and similar complications. The price, it must be observed, is derived in this way from the rent, not the rent from the price.[1] Rent is thus logically the simpler, price the more complex thing. It is well, therefore, to analyse in the first instance the principles of rent, even if we live in a country where the practice of leasing land for annual rent is less common than it is in Great Britain, even if, for whatever reason, it is the price of land with which we are concerned in practice. The problem of price contains two distinct elements which it is not easy to handle when mixed up together. For the rate of interest represents in itself an important branch of economics, which will require a separate chapter to itself.

[1] In this the rent of land differs fundamentally from that of other things, such as houses. For the price of a house is largely influenced by the costs of construction of new houses, and should correspond closely to them in the long run. The same relation between rent, price and rate of interest will hold good; but the rents will be affected by changes in the rate of interest, owing to the reactions of such changes on the supply of houses.

CHAPTER VII

RISK-BEARING AND ENTERPRISE

§ 1. *Profits and Earnings of Management.* The profits of a business, as they are ordinarily reckoned, whether for the purposes of income tax or of a balance sheet, comprise several elements which are fundamentally distinct. The relative importance of these various elements varies greatly from one type of business to another. The profits of a private business include, for instance, the remuneration of the work of management, which in the case of a Joint Stock Company is mostly paid for by salaries or directors' fees. It is to their profit that farmers, small shopkeepers, and the partners of a private firm look not merely for a return upon their capital, but for the reward of their own labours. "Earnings of Management," as they are usually termed (though in truth they often cover other and humbler forms of labour) are thus frequently one of the ingredients of profits.

§ 2. *The Payment for Risk-bearing.* There is another element of great importance about which our ordinary ideas are apt to be so vague that it will be well to devote a chapter to its examination. This is the element of payment for risk, or rather the reward of risk-bearing.

Risk is inherent in all business, as it is inherent in all life. The vagaries of nature and the vagaries of man are alike responsible. The farmer may find his harvest ruined by a drought or by a deluge; the coal or the gold, for the extraction of which you have perhaps set up an extensive mining plant, may come to an end which is unexpectedly abrupt. You may put your money into roller-skating rinks and find that cinemas have become the rage with the fickle public; sometimes "the market" may decline for causes which remain obscure but with consequences which are disagreeably plain. But while risk is always present in some degree, the degree varies enormously from one industry to another. Now, it is obvious enough that in an exceptionally risky industry, where there is a considerable possibility that the capital invested will yield no return at all, the profits of those concerns which succeed are likely to exceed the rate of interest on gilt-edged securities. But what is likely to be the magnitude of this excess? Is risk-taking rewarded if there is any such excess, however small? Or will it suffice that the gains and losses should average out to a fair rate of interest over the whole industry? To enable us to think clearly let us suppose for a moment that we can measure accurately what the chances are.

Suppose, then, that there were a precisely equal chance of success on the one hand and failure on the other in any enterprise, failure involving a complete loss of all the capital invested. Suppose, further, 6 per cent to be at the time a fair return on a perfectly secure investment. What would be the return which must be expected from the risky enterprise, in the

event of its succeeding, before it will be undertaken ?
The reader may be tempted to answer, 12 per cent.
But 12 per cent would not suffice. An equal chance
of 12 per cent or nothing, as compared with a certainty
of 6 per cent, does not mean that the risk in the former
case is paid for to the tune of 6 per cent. It means
that it is not paid for at all. In each case what a
mathematician would call the *expectation* is a return
of 6 per cent. The odds are evenly balanced ; in the
long run, over a large number of cases, if the law of
averages works as we assume it does, you would get
just as much from the one type of investment as the other.
Now, risky enterprises will not, as a rule, be undertaken
on terms like these ; investors and business men will
not take risks with the odds precisely equal ; they must
have them, or believe that they have them, in their
favour.

§ 3. *Monte Carlo and Insurance.* To assert this is not
to ignore the strength of the appeal which the gambling
instinct makes to many, if not to most of us. The
taste for gambling is, indeed, so deep and widespread
that it would be foolish to leave it out of account in this
connection. It is clear enough that at places like Monte
Carlo people are prepared to have the odds unmistakably against them, apparently for the sheer pleasure
and exhilaration of taking risks. Moreover, though for
most people play at Monte Carlo represents a mere
holiday indulgence, it would be unsafe to assume that
what appeals to them there will not also appeal to them
in their business affairs. But what exactly is the secret
of the charm of Monte Carlo ? It is the great attractive

force of a small chance of a large gain, as compared
with the deterrent force of a large chance of a small loss.
People will readily pay £1 for one chance in a hundred
of making no more, perhaps, than £80 or £90. And it
is very likely that this holds good in the world of business.
If, for example, we were to suppose that the promoters
of a new enterprise were confronted with one chance in
fifty of a profit of 50 per cent per annum on their capital,
as against forty-nine chances of a profit of 5 per cent,
this might well prove a more attractive prospect than
a certain return of 6 per cent, although the strict
expectation of profit would be smaller in the former case.
But the risks of business enterprise are not often of
this type. They conform more usually to the opposite
type of a large chance of a relatively small gain, balanced
by a small chance of serious loss or entire failure.
Now for almost everyone the possibility of great loss
will count as a deterrent (just as the possibility of a
great gain may count as an attraction) for much more
than its strict actuarial value.

The truth of this proposition is demonstrated by the
existence of institutions more impressive than Monte
Carlo—the Insurance Companies, which play so large
a part in the economic life of modern times. Every
year, and upon an ever-growing scale, both private
individuals and business concerns pay sums of
money, which reach in the aggregate a colossal
sum, as premiums to insure themselves against loss
by Fire, Shipwreck, Burglary, Death, Death Duties,
against every risk which Insurance Companies will
cover. Now Insurance Companies are not, as we say,
in business for their health. They find their business

profitable, and pay good dividends to their shareholders. Moreover, they incur a considerable expenditure on offices, on clerical staff, on agents, and the like. All these payments must be defrayed out of the premiums they receive ; so that it is plain that the premiums greatly exceed the *expectation* of the risks insured. The odds are heavily in favour of the Insurance Company—of that the stupidest person can have no shadow of doubt. Yet we continue to insure, as private individuals and as business men, and so far from being ashamed of our proceedings as a weak and nerveless folly, which somehow we are unable to resist, we blazon them forth in the strong accents of conscious pride. We preach insurance to our neighbours as the core of self-regarding duty, and, if ever we feel a twinge of uneasiness, it is lest we, too, may have omitted in some particular to practise what we preach.

The significance of this is unmistakable. Be our psychology what it may, however deep and irrepressible our taste for derring-do, however inadequate the scope which the dull routine of modern life affords for our adventurous impulses, we are most of us anxious to avoid the risk of great financial loss. We are very glad to find someone to take it off our shoulders if we can ; so glad that we are prepared to pay him for the service, to pay him a sum which covers not only the actuarial equivalent of the risk, but something substantial over and above. In this we are entirely rational. Our conduct is justified by the law of the diminishing utility of money, which was noted at the end of Chapter III. It would be plainly foolish, for instance, to substitute for the certainty of an income of £500 per annum an even chance of £1000 or nothing, since the utility to us of £1000 is not twice as great as that of £500.

The majority of business risks are not of a kind against which it is possible to insure. Insurance companies confine themselves to risks which are mainly a matter of what we call objective rather than subjective chance, i.e. risks in respect of which knowledge of detailed facts peculiar to the individual case is of minor importance. But such knowledge is of paramount importance in the case of ordinary business risks. If, for example, a new enterprise is to be undertaken, the special knowledge and experience which its promoters possess is a vital factor in determining their estimate of the risk involved. An outsider with no special knowledge would necessarily require to estimate the risk far more highly if we were to form a rational opinion on the basis of *his* knowledge. So great, indeed, would be the risk to him, that we can lay it down as a sound maxim that people are extremely rash who invest their money in risky undertakings about which they know very little. This subjective aspect of business risk has a significance to which it will be necessary to revert.

But, though most business risks are not and cannot be a matter for premiums and policies, the principle, which the practice of insurance illustrates, applies none the less. In the light of their knowledge and experience, the promoters of a new undertaking must weigh up the chances of failure and success, though they will not do so by the precise methods of an actuary. They will require that any chances of serious loss should be balanced by such chances of exceptional gain, as would

raise the *expectation* of profit well above the normal
return on secure investments. The more risky the
project seems the greater, generally speaking, must
be the *expectation* of profit required to induce people
to undertake it.

If we suppose business men to calculate reasonably,
it follows that the average profits in any industry over
a long period of years, reckoning in the losses of the
concerns which disappear altogether, are likely to be
higher, the more risky is the industry. Such a result
will not, of course, occur in every case. Even when the
calculations are reasonable, they may be entirely falsified
by the event. Moreover, business men may not calculate
reasonably on the information which they have. But,
unless we suppose their judgment to be subject to a
prevailing bias in one direction, i.e. to be unduly
optimistic as a general rule, *we* should expect, and in
any case *they* must expect, profits above the ordinary
in a risky industry.

This conclusion is sufficiently important. Far too
many people, though they admit it when it is expressly
stated and dismiss it even as a tiresome commonplace,
are apt to neglect it when the occasion for applying
it arises. For example, the great importance to any
industry of good management is generally recognized,
and the consequent desirability of paying adequate
salaries to the managerial staff. The importance
of securing a supply of capital is very widely
recognized, and the practical necessity of paying
a fair rate of interest is thus, however grudgingly,
conceded. But the "residuary profits," as they are
called, which accrue at present to the owners of a

business, are denounced in some quarters in a sweeping fashion, which seems to ignore altogether the all-pervading element of risk.   People speak as though you might appropriately limit profits in every industry to some uniform percentage on the capital employed, without making it clear whether you would even be allowed to make up in good years for the losses incurred in bad.   The effect of introducing any such crude device into our present industrial system could only be to paralyse enterprises of an unusually risky kind, which, so far from being pushed to an excess at present, are more probably curtailed unduly from the stand-point of what is socially desirable.   Like the fixing of a low maximum price for a commodity it would cause the supply to wither up and disappear.

§ 4. *Risk under Large-scale Organization.*   While this is true of the present economic system, the question is worth considering whether it represents a fundamental necessity, whether, for instance, under our world socialist commonwealth the factor of risk-bearing need play so important a part as it does in the actual business world.   This question cannot be answered with a conclusive simplicity ; opposing considerations present themselves, between which it is not easy to strike a balance.   On the one hand, in accordance with the law of averages gains and losses tend to cancel out over a large series of transactions, *when reasonable calculations have been made.*   Thus Insurance Companies, while they take heavy risks off the shoulders of policy-holders, incur relatively trifling risks themselves ; they can predict the aggregate sums which they will be called upon to pay within a small margin of error. In the same way it might seem that every enlargement of the scale of business would make for an automatic insurance and a consequent economy of risk ; and thus that if all businesses were comprised in a single financial unit, gains and losses would cancel out over so wide a range that the degree of risk remaining would be almost negligible.

This might indeed happen, if business risks were mainly of that objective kind in which the insurance companies specialize ; for then we could assume that the chances of success or failure would be estimated reasonably. But, in fact, most business risks, not being of this kind, must be estimated by processes of human judgment, which are very fallible. And here we must take account of the law of averages in another aspect, with a different bearing on the argument. When an industry comprises a large number of separate concerns, and the decisions accordingly are taken by many men, acting independently of one another, the errors of calculation will tend to some extent to cancel one another out. The undue optimism of one man will be balanced by the undue pessimism of another ; and, if there is no prevailing bias in either direction, the errors of judgment will not affect the results for the industry as a whole. But where the effective decisions are taken by very few men, the chances are far greater of a preponderating balance of error in one direction. The risks dependent on the factor of human judgment tend therefore to increase.

This truth can be illustrated by a phenomenon which is fairly familiar. It is recognized by intelligent persons that the risks of speculation in a particular commodity market or stock market increase more than proportionately to the scale of operations. A man who sets out as a " bull " upon a small scale can buy without sending up the price against him in the process, and, if he decides later that his judgment is mistaken, he can at any time cut his losses and sell out without much difficulty. But a " bull " on a very large scale cannot complete his purchases except at a price which has been raised in consequence of his own action, and he cannot count on being able to " unload " at or near the market price, should he decide to do so. If, accordingly, he miscalculates, he cannot save himself from serious loss as a smaller man might do by a prompt discovery of his error. His difficulties spring from the fundamental fact that the effects of his calculations are too great to be offset by those of the different, and often opposite, calculations of other men.

Upon the issue whether a growth in the size of the business unit is likely to diminish risk, the law of averages thus cuts both ways. The risks arising from the element of pure chance are more likely, those arising from miscalculation are less likely, to cancel out. Upon these grounds alone, it would be unsafe to conclude that there would be on balance an economy of risk under any system of national or world socialism.

§ 5. *The Entrepreneur.* There remains, however, an aspect of the problem which is perhaps more important than those discussed above. Is it probable that risks would be estimated and undertaken more wisely or less wisely under a different system of society or of

industrial organization ? Upon this issue, methods of
precise analysis are out of place, but we may have
something to learn from the emphatic testimony of
tradition. It has become an axiom of business men that,
while Governments can manage with more or less com-
petence a safe and routine business like a Postal Service,
their success would be unlikely to prove conspicuous in
undertakings where the element of risk is great. There,
it is said, we owe everything in the past to the enterprise
of individual men (for even joint-stock companies have
not been notable as pioneers) adventuring their own
fortunes in accordance with their own unfettered judgment. This contention, however much we may desire to
qualify it, has unquestionably a large measure of truth,
and the explanation is not difficult to discover. For
the wise taking of risks in industrial development of
an experimental character, peculiar conditions and
special qualities are required. First, it is necessary to
envisage distinctly the promising though risky opportunity, and this calls not infrequently for imagination
of a none too common order. Then it must be studied
with insight and expert knowledge and weighed by
processes which are as much intuitive as intellectual.
The reasons for or against taking a particular business
risk are seldom such as can adequately be expressed
in terms of arithmetic, or even by clear arguments the soundness of which is proportioned to their
logical cogency. The mysterious faculty of judgment
enters in ; and from mental processes which defy
analysis there emerge ultimately conviction and the
will to act. But it is precisely here that Government
Departments are apt to fail. It is here that the indi-

vidual, who need consult no one but himself, has a pull over any form of organization, where decisions are reached by the method of debate and agreement among a heterogeneous committee. Hence it is that we have come to regard exceptional risk-taking as the peculiar province of individual enterprise. It is probable that these deficiencies of corporate organization are tending to diminish, and it is an interesting question how far it may be found possible to eliminate them in the future.

Meanwhile the above considerations have an important bearing on the rewards which can often be obtained from risky enterprises. The number of individuals who are in a position to envisage a business opportunity, and to assess with some confidence the chances of success and failure, is very limited. Not only must they possess special knowledge, ability, imagination, confidence in their own judgment, and the capacity to act on it ; they must also have at their disposal considerable financial resources. To combine all these advantages represents a union of circumstances which is distinctly rare. The fortunate few, who do combine them, are thus generally able to extract in the form of profits a high price for their services, a price which covers not only the strict reward of risk-bearing, and the necessary remuneration of their own services, but a handsome payment for the special qualities and advantages which have been indicated. Profits, moreover, may vary between one industry and another, not only in accordance with the real risk which is entailed, but with the degree to which the supply of special knowledge, etc., is scarce or abundant.   I

This consideration goes a long way to explain the large fortunes which enterprising business men are often able to amass. It also throws some much-needed light upon the functions which such men discharge. They perform to a large extent the work of management; they supply capital on what may be a considerable scale; but it is the taking of business risk which is perhaps their most characteristic function. It is the union of these functions which distinguishes them as an essentially different type from the salaried manager who has invested his savings in rubber or in oil. In other languages there is a specific name for the man who combines all these three functions; in French he is called an "entrepreneur," in German an "Unternehmer." It is much to be regretted that in English we have no clear corresponding word. The word "capitalist" is not uncommonly employed to do duty in this connection, but this is a source of much confusion. For the word is also used, and more appropriately, to include all investors, whether or not they are active business men.

§ 6. *Risk-taking and Control.* But there is an allied confusion of more importance. We commonly suppose it to be a leading feature of our present "capitalist system" that the control of industry rests in the hands of those who supply the capital. Nor, as a general statement, is this untrue. But it conceals the essential point. Strictly speaking, it is risk-taking with which control is associated. The mere lending of money carries with it no title to control. Governments and municipalities concede no such title to the subscribers to their loans ; nor does a company to its debenture holders. The shareholders' ultimate control is based upon the fact that they bear the financial risks of the concern. Nor is this a matter of mere legal form. It is not uncommon for ordinary shares to carry with them a greater voting power than the preference shares of a corresponding value. The principle which such arrangements endeavour to express is clear : control should rest with him who bears the risk. It is with this principle rather than with a mulish insistence on the rights of property, that advocates of " workers' control " and the like have got to reckon.

§ 7. *General Analysis of Profits.* Let us conclude this chapter by clearing the ground for the next. Earnings of management, payments for risk-taking and for the special knowledge and advantages associated with it, are ingredients of the gross profits of a business. The chief element that remains is that of interest on capital. Frequently, indeed, it is not the only one. As we saw in the last chapter, a farmer may not be required by his landlord to pay the full economic rent for his farm ; and he may therefore make profits above the normal level, above the ordinary return for his own services, his own capital expenditure, and the risks to which he is necessarily exposed. In such a case the farmer is really the recipient, as we have already suggested, of part of the economic rent of the land ; and an element of rent accordingly enters into his gross profits. But profits may include a surplus element which may arise in a great variety of other ways. A business may possess some decided advantage which is not open to

competitors ; and it may reap high profits accordingly
You can, for instance, if you choose, regard the high
money profits, which, as was suggested in Chapter IV,
are likely to accrue in future to the owners of pre-war
factories, as a surplus profit of this kind. But while, as
this illustration indicates, the phenomenon of surplus
profits becomes of very great importance when we seek
to study the distribution of wealth, it need not detain
us here. For the surplus element arises only in so far
as the costs of a business are lower than the marginal
costs ; and it is the marginal costs, which, with good
reason, we are now endeavouring to analyse. The
marginal costs must include a normal profit, i.e. a
profit which will cover earnings of management, the
reward of risk and enterprise, interest on capital,
but nothing further. It remains, then, only to consider
this last element of interest.

CHAPTER VIII

CAPITAL

§ 1. *A Reference to Marx.* Interest is the price paid simply for the use of capital. But what is capital, and in what does its use consist ? What claim has it to be regarded as an independent factor of production ? Our very familiarity with the term, our habit of employing it with the rich looseness of every-day life is an obstacle to the clearness of thought, which is again essential. We recognize, most of us, clearly enough that capital, although we reckon it in terms of money, consists, like income, of real things ; factories, machinery, materials and the like. It is quite obvious that these things are of use, are, indeed, indispensable for production ; what more natural than that capital should command a price ? It almost seems as though we might pass, without further ado, to a detailed discussion of the forces which determine the amount of this price.

But this account does not bring out the essential point, as a brief reference to a very famous controversy will show. Some ingenious writers in the last century, the most notable of whom was Karl Marx, set out to prove that, in our modern society, workpeople are "exploited," robbed of the "whole produce of their labour," to the full extent of the return which accrues to capital. The argument was exceedingly complex in detail; but it boils down to this : The factories and machinery which are admittedly essential to production were themselves produced in exactly the same way as consumable goods. They were produced by labour, working with the assistance of nature, and, again, if you choose, of capital in the form of further factories, machinery, etc. But these further capital goods can in their turn be regarded as the product of labour, nature and capital : and so we can proceed until it seems as though the element of capital must disappear in the last analysis, as though labour and nature were the sole ultimate agents of production, and the reward of capital represented no more than the exercise of the exploiter's power. In one form or another this argument still dominates the minds of a large proportion of the so-called "rebels" against the existing social order.

If we are to meet this argument, if, which is perhaps more important, we are to understand the true nature of capital, we cannot rest content with saying that it consists of factories and machinery, and that these are essential to the worker. Just as it was well to get behind the money terms, in which we often think of capital, to the real goods ; so we have now to get behind the real goods to something else. What this something else is, the first chapter may have already done something to reveal.

§ 2. *Waiting for Production.* Between production and consumption there is an interval of time. All productive processes take time to accomplish. The farmer must plough the soil and sow the seed months before he can reap the harvest which will reward him for his efforts. Meanwhile, he must live, and in order that he may live he must consume. If he employs labourers he must pay them wages, that they too may consume and live. For both purposes he requires purchasing power, which represents of course command over real things ; and if he has not sufficient purchasing power of his own, he must borrow from someone else who has. In either case it is not enough that the farmer and his labourers should work ; no less essential is it that someone should *wait*. The farmer must wait till he has sold his crops, both for the reward of his own labour and for the repayment of the wages he advances in the meantime to his labourers. Or, if he cannot afford to wait, and borrows in anticipation of the harvest, then the lender must wait, until the farmer, having sold his crop, is able to repay him. Thus the period of time involved in all production gives rise to a demand for *waiting*, which someone or other must supply, if the production is to take place. It is this waiting which is the essential reality underlying the phenomena of capital and interest. It is really this which constitutes an independent factor of production, distinct from labour and nature, and equally necessary.

§ 3. *Waiting for Consumption*. But let us carry the argument a step further. After the farmer has sold his crops, there are many stages through which they must pass, at each of which more waiting is required, before they reach the ultimate consumer. But then the waiting is at an end.

This, however, is by no means the case with a great number of commodities. Let us take the case of a speculative builder (a species, in Great Britain, now unhappily extinct). While he is building a house he, like the farmer, must wait (or find someone to wait on his behalf) for his own reward, and for the repayment of his expenditure on wages and materials. But, after the house is built, if he lets it to a tenant for an annual rent, his waiting is far from over. Not until many years have passed will the rent payments add up to a sum which equals or exceeds his outlay. He may, of course, sell the house, and thus bring his waiting to an end. But then the purchaser must wait, no matter whether or not he is the occupier. For no one would consider the use of a house for a day, a month, or a year as an adequate return for the price it cost to buy. The occupier-owner pays for the prospect of its use for a long and perhaps indefinite number of years ahead, and he must wait to enjoy the benefits for which he pays now in full. Waiting is as inherent in the consumption of durable things as it is in all production.

Now most industries are consumers of durable things of a very expensive kind. Here we come back to the factories and machinery which ordinarily spring to our mind at the mention of the word capital. Not merely does the construction of these things involve waiting; their consumption involves waiting on a vastly larger scale. Just as with a house, many years must elapse before their derived utility can even approximate to their purchase price. It is mainly to supply the waiting involved in the consumption of such durable goods, that a typical joint-stock company issues shares for public subscription. The waiting required to cover the period of time, which its own productive process requires, is largely supplied by means of bank overdrafts or other forms of short-period borrowing. More strictly, fixed capital represents the waiting involved in the consumption of durable things ; circulating capital the waiting involved in current production.

This distinction loses its sharpness when we consider not the affairs of a particular business, but the industrial system as a whole. Then the period of time involved in the consumption of durable instruments falls into place as part of the time required for the production of the ultimate consumers' goods. We can even, perhaps, conceive of an "average period of production" for industry and commerce as a whole ; and this conception is not without its uses. For it serves to bring out the fact that the period of consumption, and the period of production in the narrower sense, are only two aspects of the same fundamental thing, the interval of time which elapses between work and the utility, which is its ultimate purpose. It serves, moreover, to make clear that anything which lengthens this interval of time increases the demand for waiting, or in other words, the demand for capital ; and, conversely, that anything which shortens this interval diminishes the demand for capital.

§ 4. *Capital not a Stock of Consumable Goods.* But the distinction between the two forms of waiting, though not fundamental, is none the less worth noting. It enables us to keep our theory in conformity with fact, to look at the phenomenon of capital the right

way up ; and it is easy, if we are not careful, to slip
into the habit of looking at it upside down. People
sometimes speak as though the commodities which
constitute our capital, instead of being mainly, as our
plain sense tells us that they are, factories, machinery
and other durable instruments, were rather a *store* or
stock of immediately consumable goods. The argument
takes the following form. It is consumers' goods,
things like food and clothes, which the farmer, the builder
and their workpeople consume while they are working.
To enable them to work, therefore, it is vital that such
things should not in the past have been consumed
as soon as they were made ; part of them must have
been saved, and carried forward for future use. Furthermore, the longer the time that the work on which people
are now engaged takes to yield its product, the larger
must be this store of consumers' goods. For these
products, when they are completed, will serve (taking
society as a whole) to replace the store which in the
meantime is being used up, so that the longer this
replacement takes, the larger must be the initial store.
Conversely, the larger the store of consumers' goods
available, the more distant is the future for which we
can afford to work. It is thus the store or stock of
consumers' goods which represents our real capital ;
for it is the magnitude of this store which determines
how far we can devote our energies to purposes which
are remote in time.

Now this is pure mysticism. Regarded literally,
it is in direct conflict with the facts. The processes
of industry are fairly regular and continuous. At any
moment, large quantities of consumers' goods of almost

every kind are on the point of completion ; at the same moment equally large quantities are consumed. The things which we buy were finished, very likely, only recently ; or, if in fact they have lain idle for some time in stock, there is nothing essential or at all helpful in that fact. It represents rather a defect—a maladjustment which should be rectified. Even many kinds of agricultural produce do not need to be carried forward from one year to another, for they are produced in many parts of the world, where the seasons come at different periods of the year. It is conceivable, therefore, that we might consume all non-durable things the moment they were ready, and the degree to which we approximate to this ideal is a mark of the efficiency of our economic system. A large store of consumable goods is thus *not* a fundamental necessity of a prosperous society.

What *is* necessary is plainly the power to produce these things in large quantities as they are required. And this power is furnished by the durable instruments of production, which we thus rightly regard as the true representatives of modern capital. If it is argued that this power to produce consumable goods may be regarded as being *in effect* a store of consumable goods, it must be sternly replied that this is the language of symbolism, not of science, and that symbolism is highly dangerous in this connection. The false conception of capital as essentially a store of consumers' goods has led and still leads to many serious fallacies. It was this that gave rise to the notorious doctrine of the Wages Fund ; the notion that the sum which can at any time be paid in wages is equal to the quantity of capital, *alias* consumable goods, which happens to exist. To this day it blocks, with an undergrowth of obscurantist controversies, the way to a straightforward account of the problem of trade cycles.

§ 5. *The Essence of Waiting.* But it is with positive conclusions that we must here concern ourselves. What is the essence of this waiting, as we have called it ? What are its results from the point of view of the community ? The individual, who saves and lends, waits in the obvious sense that he postpones consumption. He forgoes his right to purchase now a quantity of consumers' goods in consideration of the prospect of purchasing a larger quantity of such things in the future. From the standpoint of the whole community, there is a similar postponement of consumption, though it need not commence so soon. The store of consumable goods is what it is : the quantity of goods in *process* of manufacture, which will shortly be coming forward, is also what it is. For some time, therefore, a sudden access of saving cannot affect the quantity of goods available for consumption ; and if, in fact, they should be consumed less rapidly, that will represent an unfortunate defect, not an essential condition of a smoothly working system. The *necessary* consequence comes later. The increased saving will cause labour, materials, land, agents of production generally, to be devoted to distant purposes. Men will be set to work producing durable goods, largely durable instruments of production like ships or railways or factories or plant. If the increased saving is considerable, the labour, materials, etc., required for these purposes will be withdrawn even under

our present system, as under a smoothly working
system they clearly must be, from the production of
other and more immediately consumable things. Hence,
some time later, the supplies of consumable things will
be diminished, while at a later period still they will
be more than correspondingly increased as the result
of the assistance of the new durable instruments.
That is the essence of saving from the social standpoint. An early future is sacrificed to a more remote
future. The aggregate consumable income of the present
is unaffected; the aggregate consumable income of the
near future is actually diminished; it is not until at
least some years later that the aggregate consumable
income is increased.

§ 6. *Individual and Social Saving.* This conclusion
is important: but there is an obvious misinterpretation
against which it will be well to guard. It is customary
for social moralists to preach thrift and saving as a
public duty, and to impart to their appeals a special
note of urgency in times like the immediate post-war
years when, as the result of the havoc of the war, destitu-
tion was widespread over Europe. Now obviously the
authors of such appeals did not mean to recommend
something which would impoverish the world in the
next year and the year after, and the benefit of which
would accrue only in a distant future: it was the immediate urgency of the world's needs which was the
substance of their case. Nor would it be right to conclude that these wise men were the victims of a delusion,
and advocated a course, the consequences of which they
did not understand. The explanation of the paradox

is simple. The more the community as a whole saves now, the less in the near future will be the aggregate consumable income of the whole community : but not of the *remainder* of the community, exclusive of the savers. It is the saver who must wait, whose consumption must be postponed to perhaps a distant future ; but *at no time* does his saving result in a smaller income of consumable goods for other people. The aggregate consumable income of the near future will be dimished, but it may be better distributed, and it may consist of things of a different *kind*. For consumers' goods, we must remember, comprise champagne and motor-cars as well as food and clothes ; and, if a rich man saves, it may be purely articles of luxury, the production of which will shortly be diminished. Moreover, if his saving has the effect of transferring purchasing power to impoverished people, like those in Central Europe after the Armistice, it will not be devoted to a distant future ; it will very likely be devoted to quite immediate ends. In other words, it may not result in any " creation of capital " ; it may not represent any saving on the part of the community as a whole. A relatively rich man waits (even a British artisan may be relatively rich in this connection), and a relatively poor man *anticipates* his income to a corresponding extent ; and it is precisely this that is so urgently desirable in a time of widespread poverty and chaos.

This is no matter of hair-splitting, and making plain things obscure. While it is always better for the *rest* of us that an individual, who can afford to save, should save rather than spend (though it might be better for us still if we could have his money to spend ourselves) and while this is the more important the greater is the poverty which generally prevails; yet, as a community we cannot save so much, we *ought* not to save so much, when we are impoverished as when we are prosperous. It is vital to appreciate this truth, because, as we shall see, by no means all the saving of the world is done by individuals. There are many forms of "collective saving," which take place in actual fact; still more which we are often urged to undertake. And it is of practical importance to realize that the very considerations, which call most urgently for individual thrift, forbid a great indulgence in such projects. A time of national poverty is not a time when it is suitable for the State to embark on large schemes of capital development: we require our resources for more immediate ends. Faced with such problems, our practical sense may no doubt suffice to keep us straight; but it is apt to do so at the expense of a complete inversion of the real issues. If, for instance, we call for Governmental retrenchment on what we deem extravagant policies of housing and education, we usually speak as though they represented the profligacy of a spendthrift as contrasted with the saving that is indispensable. The truth is rather that these policies represent a saving, an investment for future purposes, which may conceivably be greater than the community can properly afford. This is another instance of what I mean by looking at the problem of capital the right way up.

§ 7. *The Necessity of Interest.* It is only now that we are in a position to appreciate the true functions of a rate of interest, and the nature of its claims to be regarded as a " real cost." Interest, it is sometimes said is necessary to provide for the future. It is far more certain that interest is necessary to provide for the present. It is a matter of legitimate doubt how far it is necessary to *pay* interest to secure a supply of capital ; there is no doubt at all that it is necessary to *charge* interest to limit the demand for it. As we saw in Chapter I, a world socialist commonwealth would require to retain a rate of interest, if only as a matter of book-keeping, in order to choose between the various capital undertakings that were technically possible. And this is the primary function which the rate of interest fulfils in our present-day society. It separates the sheep from the goats. It serves as a screen, by means of which capital projects are sifted, and through which only those are allowed to pass which will benefit the future in a high degree. For this essential purpose it is hard to imagine how a better instrument could be devised.

§ 8. *The Supply of Capital.* Let us dwell for a moment on this image of a screen, or sieve. One condition of a good sieve is that its meshes should all be of the same size. This condition the rate of interest almost perfectly fulfils. But it is also important that the meshes should be of the *right* size. Whether this is true of the actual rate of interest is a far more doubtful matter. It is, indeed, plain that it is not altogether devoid of merit in this respect. In times of general world poverty, like those which follow upon a great war, it is desirable, as has been argued, that more of our productive resources

should be devoted to immediately useful purposes, and
a smaller portion dedicated to a distant future. This
readjustment the rate of interest helps to bring about.
For it rises to a higher level, and there is accordingly
a strong inducement to all manufacturers and traders
to economize their use of capital, and thus to set free
productive resources for more urgent needs. But,
while the meshes of the sieve, as it were, contract in
times when it is desirable that they should contract,
we have no reason for supposing that they will contract
in just the degree that is desired, neither more nor less ;
or, indeed, that at any time they approximate to the
right size. We in the twentieth century owe much
of the material wealth that we enjoy to the fact that
over the last century men saved as largely as they
did. But our natural gratitude should not restrain
us from doubting whether they were really well advised
to do so. If we ask the question *how* they managed to
do so, our doubts are deepened. For first place among
the explanations must be assigned to the inequality
in the then distribution of wealth. It was because
many men in England were rich enough to save that our
railways were built, and the resources of new Continents
were opened up. But England, a century or even half a
century ago, was not really a rich community. And if
the national income in those days had been distributed
more evenly among the people, can we doubt that they
would have spent a far larger proportion of it on
immediate needs ; can we doubt that they would have
been right to do so ? We may rather doubt, in view
of the reactions of poverty on physical and mental
efficiency, on social harmony, even possibly on population,

K

whether we to-day would have been really injured
as much as might appear. How, then, can we suppose
that the sum of the amounts which it suits individuals
to save will bear any close relation to the resources
which the community can properly devote to future
ends ? Are we to regard an unjust distribution of wealth
as a mysterious dispensation of Providence for securing
perfect harmony between the future and the present ?
The point need not be laboured further. There are no
grounds for assuming that we save, as a community,
even roughly what we ought to save. If we wish to
believe we do, we must turn for support from economics
to theology.

It is important to be clear upon this issue in order to
distinguish it from another, with which it sometimes
seems to be confused. This is the question, briefly
outlined in Chapter II, of the effect of changes in the
rate of interest on the supply of capital. As was there
indicated, there are good reasons for supposing that a
fall in the rate of interest would induce some people
to save more, and conversely. But the balance of probability is in favour of the conclusion that the *net* effect
of changes in the rate of interest, though perhaps slight,
is usually of the more ordinary kind. The decisive argument in this connection is the fact, upon which we have
just touched, that savings are supplied largely by people
who are relatively rich, and who become richer when
the rate of interest rises. For at this point it is necessary
to be careful. It is easy to slide from the above conclusion into an argument of the following kind. A higher
rate of interest leads to more saving ; it is thus necessary
to *evoke* more saving ; it is thus required as an *incentive*

to induce people to incur the *sacrifice* of waiting; this sacrifice represents the "real cost" for which interest is paid.

This terminology of incentive, inducement and sacrifice is of very dubious validity. A rich man, who is made richer by a rise in the rate of interest, will probably save more, but it will be rather because he has become richer than because he is tempted by the higher rate : and the less we talk about his sacrifice the better. Nor is it clear that the attraction of a high rate of interest is an operative factor on the mind of a man to whom saving means a real sacrifice of immediate comfort or enjoyment. Certainly it is only one among many factors, and seldom an important one. A really poor man will think not so much of the annual income which will accrue from his savings, as of the capital sum upon which he or his family can fall back if a rainy day should come. And for this purpose he might save as much as he saves now, even if there were no interest to be obtained thereby. He might even be prepared to lend what he had saved, at least to banks (a deposit with a bank is in effect a loan), for the mere advantage of safe custody. The people who save rather for the sake of the capital sum that can be realized than for that of the annual interest are very numerous, and probably include many men in receipt of quite considerable earned incomes. Moreover, those who consider mainly the future annual income which their savings will yield them, are usually more concerned with its absolute amount than with the ratio it bears to the amount they must save in order to acquire it. For this reason, as has been often recognized, they may save less when the rate of interest rises, since a smaller quantity of savings will ensure to them the future annual income they desire to obtain. There is no need to be dogmatic upon any of these points. The psychology of saving is both complex and obscure. Our conclusion must be the negative one that we have insufficient evidence to warrant the assertion that the particular rate of interest which happens to prevail is a measure of the sacrifice involved in saving, even in the case of what we might regard as the "marginal saving." And, if we cannot assert this, we must be careful not to assume it as the basis of other arguments, or as part of a general analysis of price or exchange value.

It is of some interest to observe that the difficulties which our world socialist commonwealth would encounter if it attempted to dispense with the rate of interest, would not necessarily include that of obtaining a supply of capital. It might, indeed, not find it easy to determine the proportions in which it should allocate its productive resources between immediate and distant ends. Our present system cannot be said to have evolved satisfactory principles for the solution of this question ; and the socialist commonwealth would have to work out its own solution. But when it directed that labour and materials should be devoted to purposes of long-period utility, there would be an automatic collective saving, of which no one would be conscious as an individual sacrifice. Even at the present time, our capital is not supplied entirely by the savings of individuals, but to an extent which appears from the calculations of the Colwyn Committee to amount in Great Britain to over two-fifths of the whole, by involuntary saving of an essentially similar type to the above.

§ 9. *Involuntary Saving.* When a municipality embarks on a municipal tramways scheme or any other industrial enterprise, and pays off by means of a sinking-fund the capital which it borrows in the first instance, the proceeding amounts, as the defenders of municipal trading have rightly claimed, to a compulsory and unconscious saving on the part of the citizens. Their consumption has been postponed willy-nilly as the result of the increased rates or the high charges which they have had to pay ; and, when the subscribers to the original loan have been paid off, the capital of the community is enhanced to the extent of that loan. Central governments might similarly increase the supply of capital by devoting annual revenue to capital purposes; though their actual record, as it happens, is mainly of a different kind. But what is chiefly a possibility in the case of Governments has actually been carried out on an enormous scale by other institutions. The development of the joint-stock company system has introduced a new factor into the problem of the supply of capital, which is of immense though but dimly perceived importance. The directors of a company are technically no more than the servants of the shareholders. It is the profit of the shareholders that it is the directors' duty to promote with a single mind. and the whole capital of the concern, including its reserves both open and concealed, is the shareholders' exclusive property. But realities have a way of differing from forms, and just as in political affairs it is common to regard the State as a very different thing to the people who compose it, as a sublime entity with a separate existence of its own, so directors and managers of a

large public company are apt to distinguish between
the company and the shareholders. To pay away
in dividends to shareholders money which they could
employ in extending the business or strengthening the
position of the company appears to some directors a
necessity hardly less unpleasant than an increased
wages bill, or an Excess Profits Duty. Concessions must
indeed be made to the shareholders' rapacity : but
when something has been done in this direction, dust
can easily be thrown in their not very observant eyes.
Reserves, which within limits are a necessity of sound
finance, can be accumulated beyond those limits, and,
when the further limits of an extreme but just arguable
conservatism have been passed, there remain the
innumerable devices, known to every resourceful
Board, of hidden reserves, the secret of which is un-
menaced by the meagre information of a balance-sheet.
In all this the shareholder, as the directors occasionally
assure themselves, has no real grievance, for he will
gain in the long run, from the appreciation in the capital
value of his shares, all and perhaps more than all that
he foregoes in the meantime in the way of dividends.

In the long run the shareholder is not injured ; but
in the meantime he is in effect compelled, without
any consciousness of the proceeding, to save and to
reinvest in the company a portion of the dividends,
which he might otherwise have spent. The reserves
which are accumulated are not allowed to lie idle :
they are employed either in what are really capital
extensions of the business, or in the purchase of outside
securities, and in either case they represent an increase
in the total supply of capital. The principle which

these proceedings represent is capable of indefinite
extension.

But however possible it might be to secure a supply
of capital without the inducement of a rate of interest,
that rate is indispensable for dealing with the demand.
It is no good saying, " Three per cent seems a fair rate
of interest ; let us try and limit it to that." Given
the amount of savings which are supplied, the rate of
interest must be allowed to reach whatever figure
is necessary to confine the demand to that amount.
Given the quantity of resources which you have available
for future needs, the meshes of the sieve must be made
as narrow as is necessary to confine the projects that
pass through within those limits. And so, indeed, it
becomes necessary for any particular business to pay
for its capital interest at the market rate, not so much
to secure the saving of it as to secure its allocation from
the common pool.

§ 10. *Interest and Distribution.* It is unavoidable that
this interest should accrue to whomever it is that
supplies the capital. As things are, the capital is
supplied mainly by the savings of individuals, and
largely by individuals confined to a relatively narrow
class. The profits of Capital have thus a vital influence
on the very serious matter of the distribution of
wealth between social classes. Now, as experience
shows, there is no element in profits which is capable
of such radical change in so short a space of time,
as is the rate of interest. Even before the war it had
become hard for people in Great Britain to realize
that 3 per cent Consols had stood at 114 as late as

1896. " How blest," wrote two cynical satirists of
society in the same period :

> " How blest the prudent man, the maiden pure,
> Whose income is both ample and secure,
> Arising from Consolidated Three
> Per cent Annuities, paid quarterly."[1]

It is impossible to read those lines now without a
sense of irony, different from that which they were
intended to convey.

Since the 'nineties a much higher rate of interest has
prevailed, particularly during the post-war decade.
This higher rate of interest is not attributable to any
decline in the habit of thrift, nor to any abnormal demand for capital for ordinary industrial purposes. It
is mainly due to the large scale upon which Governments throughout the world have borrowed money for
purposes mostly unproductive and mostly connected
with war—to finance preparations for war, to conduct
war, or to repair the destruction and to deal with the
problems resulting from war. If it should prove that we
have now entered upon a more peaceful era, in which
swords will absorb a smaller part of our savings, and
leave a large part available for ploughshares, the rate
of interest may be expected to decline. It is even
possible that 3 per cent may come again before long to
be regarded as a very satisfactory return upon a really
gilt-edged security. Such a change would exert a fundamental and powerful influence in the direction of a
lower level of business profits, and of greater equality
in the distribution of wealth.

[1] *Narcissus*, by Samuel Butler and Henry Festing Jones.

CHAPTER IX

LABOUR

§ 1. *A Retrospect on Laissez-faire.* When, a century and a half ago, the foundations were being laid in the Western world of systematic economic theory, the public attention was much occupied with a subject, which indeed has not ceased to hold it : that of the failings of Governments. The general interest in that topic was shared by the pioneers of economic thought, of whom, in Great Britain, Adam Smith was the most notable. It was indeed their practical concern with the concrete economic issues of the day which very naturally gave the impetus to their scientific quest. It was hardly less natural that they should have expressed their opinions on these concrete issues with considerable emphasis.

Now the keynote of their practical conclusions was that Governments were doing immense mischief by meddling with a great many matters, which they would have done better to leave alone. In this they were in general agreement with one another ; incidentally— let there be no mistake about it—they were right. But, as invariably happens in public controversy, their opinions became crystallized in a compact formula, or cry, with unduly sweeping implications. This was the

cry of "*laissez-faire.*" Let Governments preserve law
and order ; and leave the economic sphere alone. The
economists picked no quarrel with this formula ; it
served well enough for workaday purposes to indicate the
lines of policy which they rightly thought essential in
their day.

The history of this cry is the history of every cry
which has won a wide acceptance from mankind. It did
good work for perhaps half a century ; but then many
crimes were committed in its name. The instrument
which had been forged to clear away a noxious tariff
jungle and the monstrous laws of Settlement, was
turned against Lord Shaftesbury and the Factory Acts.
Not only was inaction recommended to Governments
as the highest wisdom ; other institutions, like trade
unions, were warned off the economic grass. An ideal
of perfect competition became an idol to which much
human flesh and blood were sacrificed.

But, what is more to our present purpose, the idea
took root of an intimate association between the laws
of economics and the policy of *laissez-faire.* People
who opposed some long-overdue measure of State
regulation believed themselves to be justified by the
eternal verities of economic law, and this claim even
the advocates of the measure seldom ventured to
dispute. They took refuge rather in a conception of
economic law as a dangerous monster, whose claws
must be clipped in the interests of the higher good.
This notion that all interference with so-called "free
competition," is a violation (though very likely fully
justified) of economic laws has sunk deep into our
common thought. So that to this day, whenever we

see at work the hand of a State department, a trust or
a trade union, we are apt to say "Demand and supply
are here in abeyance," and possibly we add "A good
thing too." Since in the matter of wages, the hand of
the trade union is very generally evident, it is impossible
to discuss the subject-matter of this chapter, until we
have rid our minds of this quite baseless prepossession.

To sweep away this cobweb, I urge the reader to
recall here the general tenor of the analysis of the
preceding chapters. Whether we were dealing with the
price of an ordinary commodity, with joint products,
land or capital, we came across relationships which
seemed altogether more fundamental than our present
industrial system; nor, we may incidentally observe,
were we ever required to suppose that the present
system was one of "perfect competition." These
relationships were almost invariably such that even a
world socialist commonwealth would find it necessary
to maintain them. It was not suggested, and most
certainly it must not be thought, that a world socialist
commonwealth, or even a more modest remodelling of
the social order would not effect great changes, possibly
for good, and possibly for ill. The same economic laws
might be made to bear very different fruits, but they
themselves would remain unchanged. What is true in all
these other fields—this should be our predisposition—is
not likely to be quite untrue in the field of labour.

§ 2. *Ideas and Institutions.* Another point is worth
noting here. We are sometimes advised to distinguish
sharply between "What should be" and "What is";
often two very different things. The advice is pertinent

and useful, particularly in the sphere of sociology. But
our incorrigible habit of confusing the two things
together is not without justification, or at least excuse.
For, in fact, they gravitate towards one another with a
force which is just as strong as the capacity of man for
understanding and controlling his environment. When
we have a system which is clearly bad, *and* when we see
our way to make it better, we generally make the change
however tardily. Our sense of " What should be " thus
reacts upon " What is." Meanwhile, until we can make
the system better, our appreciation of " What is "
affects our sense of " What should be." And the more
so, as we are sensible. For " What should be " is
pre-eminently an affair of relativity. A man may
hold very strongly that equal pay to every individual
is desirable, as he puts it, as an ideal. But this will not
prevent him, in a world in which managers are paid far
more than manual workers, from maintaining hotly
(at any rate, if he is sensible) that to pay the manager of
a particular concern a manual worker's wage would
be monstrously unfair. He would also argue that it
would be highly inexpedient. Equity and expediency
are, in fact, intricately intertwined in our sense of
" What should be " ; and our sense of " What should
be " in the particular is governed by our knowledge of
" What is " in the general.

These may seem unnecessary commonplaces. But they
have a vital bearing on the *modus operandi* of economic
laws. These laws do not work *in vacuo*. They work
through the medium of the acts of men. The acts of
men are greatly influenced by their institutions, and by
their ideas of right and wrong. Both institutions and

ideas may serve to smooth rather than obstruct the
path of economic laws; because the laws may
represent either "what should be" in the general,
or "what is" in the general, and therefore "what
should be" in the particular. This may hold true
even of a trade union or a sense of "fair wages."
The business of economic theory is not to justify a
régime of *laissez-faire*, still less to show the folly of
bringing morals into business. Its value is rather that
it may help us, by improving our understanding, to
shape our institutions, and to adapt our moral senti-
ments so as to promote the public welfare. With these
general notions in our minds, let us turn to see how
stands the case with Labour.

§ 3. *The General Wage Level.* The term Labour may be
used in a broad or in a narrow sense. It may be confined
to weekly wage-earners : it may be extended to include
all those who work, as the phrase goes, "with either
hand or brain." It is with all classes of Labour, in the
broadest sense of the term, that we must here concern
ourselves. It will be convenient, however, in the first
instance to ignore the differences between them, and to
consider the forces which determine what we may
regard as the general wage-level.

The general laws of supply and demand hold good.
The wages of labour tend to a level at which the demand
is equal to the supply. For, if the demand exceeds the
supply, if, in other words, labour is scarce, wages tend
to rise, sooner or later in any case, and the more promptly
in proportion as the workpeople are organized. Conversely, if the supply exceeds the demand, if in other

words there is general unemployment, wages tend to fall, and the strongest trade unions cannot resist the tendency, though they may delay it. Moreover, the higher the wages that must be paid, the smaller, other things being equal, is the demand for labour. For, even if we leave foreign competition out of account, and consider, as it were, labour throughout the world as a whole, the demand for labour is by no means inelastic. It is derived along with the demand for the other agents of production in the manner described in Chapter V. from the demand for consumers' goods. As was there shown, the greater the supply of the other agents of production, the greater is likely to be the demand for labour; but these other agents can be substituted for labour in a great variety of ways, and an increase in wages (unless accompanied by increased efficiency) will make it profitable for employers to effect such a substitution, where it was not profitable before. Thus, higher wages for the same labour efficiency must stimulate the tendency for capital to act as a substitute for labour at the expense necessarily (since the aggregate supply of capital will not be increased thereby) of its tendency to serve as a complement; and this must mean a decrease in the volume of employment. Hence the power of labour to secure a general advance of wages by concerted or simultaneous trade union action, applied if you will, not merely to every industry, but to every country, is necessarily very limited. Beyond a certain point, such a policy must result in general unemployment; and, if pushed sufficiently far, in unemployment so extensive that it would continue even in periods of active trade. Such a policy could neither be maintained in practice nor would it be a wise policy from the workers' point of view.

In other words, given on the one hand the conditions of the demand for labour (i.e. the supply of capital, natural resources, business ability, risk-bearing and knowledge of technical processes, etc., which happens to exist), and given on the other hand the supply of labour (i.e. both the numbers of workpeople and their efficiency), the wage-level in the long run is fairly rigidly determined. The introduction of the phrase " in the long run " in this connection is apt to provoke comment which may be pertinent, but may be misconceived. The worker, it is pointed out, is deeply concerned with " the short run " in which he has to live. It is very true ; and it is this that supplies one of the many justifications of trade unionism. To secure for the workers advances of wages, which economic conditions justify, sooner than would otherwise have been obtained, is certainly no trivial or contemptible function. But it is none the less an illusion to suppose that the general wage-level can be appreciably and permanently raised by trade union action, except in so far as it increases the efficiency of the workers or incidentally stimulates the efficiency of the employers.

§ 4. *The Supply of Labour in General.* The efficiency of labour may be regarded as affecting either the demand for labour on the one hand or the supply of it on the other, according as we look at the matter from the worker's or the employer's standpoint. The employer is concerned with the labour costs per unit of his output, the worker is concerned with the wages he receives.

An increase in the efficiency of labour may, and usually will, mean both a decrease in labour costs to the employer and an increase in the earnings of the worker. It is thus wholly to the good. But the effects of an increase in the supply of labour in the sense of a growth in the numbers of the population are far more dubious. Unaccompanied by an increase in the *demand* for labour, it *must* result in a diminished remuneration for the individual worker. To some extent indeed the demand for labour would almost certainly be increased. The supply of Capital may expand, perhaps proportionately, perhaps more than proportionately to the increase in population. But one factor of production, as we have seen, is not capable of such expansion. This is the factor of Land, or Natural Resources. It is the limitation of this factor which gives rise to what we have most of us heard of as The Law of Diminishing Returns. It is this that is the essence of the problem of Population, portrayed in sombre hues more than a hundred years ago by Malthus.

This problem will form the subject of a separate volume of the present series. In the meantime it may be suggested that we are easily credulous if we suppose that the problem has been finally disposed of by the peculiar progress of an abnormal century. But that experience has at least destroyed the view that there *need be*, or even is in fact in Western countries, a relation between real wages and the numbers of the people so close and direct that an improved standard of living must be temporary only, doomed to destroy itself by the increased population it engenders. One may perhaps go further and say that it is doubtful even in what direction changes in remuneration will influence the aggregate supply of labour. When we pass to "what should be," it is plain that there is nothing whatever to be said for the sort of relation indicated above. The view once widely held that the principle of population must inevitably keep the mass of people close to the verge of the bare means of subsistence was no statement of a desirable ideal. It was a nightmare. It is far from fanciful to suggest that it is because this relation is so obviously *not* "what should be" that it may be ceasing to hold true in fact. But it would be very fanciful indeed to maintain that as yet "what should be" is represented by the actual population. Thus, just as with capital, so with labour, there is no reason to suppose that the aggregate supply is determined by any fundamental economic law, or corresponds in practice to what is socially desirable.

§ 5. *The Apportionment of Labour among Places*. Again, as with capital, it is when we turn to the *apportionment* of labour between different employments that both economic law and social ideal make their appearance. It will be well, however, to consider briefly in the first instance the different question of its apportionment between places. This was hardly necessary in the case of capital, because the possibilities of foreign investment are very numerous and easy : the mobility of capital is thus sufficiently strong (once again it is only *marginal* adjustment that is necessary) to establish over at least a large part of the world something near to a uniform rate of interest. But this is not the case with

L

labour. People do indeed move from place to place within a country, and from one country to another, in response to economic opportunities. That even the latter movement may be a considerable thing, the present population of the United States is a striking testimony. But obviously the mobility is very incomplete. Here, then, we have what we might *loosely* call an economic law that labour tends to " flow " (as it is sometimes unhappily phrased) to those places where it can command the highest reward ; we have this tendency in evidence, but it is far too weak to enable us to lay down what would deserve more strictly the title of an economic law, that in the long run the reward of the same kind of labour is roughly equal in all places. Perhaps we can say this for many districts in a single country ; but for few countries is this true as between all their districts. As between countries, it is not remotely true.

Here, however, the imperfection of economic law is balanced by an extreme uncertainty as to the ideal. Perfect mobility of labour may be *economically* desirable in a very narrow sense of the term ; but it opens out a vista of racial, national and cultural problems, into which it will be better for us not to enter here. We must take for granted the population of a country, like that of the world, as a given fact.

When we do this, the question of its remuneration is on all fours with the more general question discussed above. That the remuneration of the labour of a country is mainly governed by the relations between demand and supply is an inexorable fact. In view of the international mobility of capital, the main

distinctive factor in the demand for the labour of a particular country is the supply of natural resources, which
it knows how to use.   Where the natural resources are
great relatively to the population, there wages will
rule high ; where the converse is true, wages will rule
low.   This result of economic analysis is abundantly
confirmed by experience.   The relatively high wages in
the new world, the low standard of living in the densely
populated East ; the economic history of Ireland are so
many object-lessons of its truth.

§ 6.   *The Apportionment of Labour among Social Grades.*
The question of the apportionment of the labour of a
country among different employments falls under two
heads.   Some differences of occupation are associated
particularly in Great Britain with differences of what
we know as class.   The movement of labour between
different social grades is clearly a very different thing
from its movement between different occupations in the
same grade.   The grades themselves are not easy to
define : not a little ingenuity has been expended on the
attempt, and perhaps the best brief classification that
has been put forward is one which divides labour into the
following four grades :—

    (1) Automatic manual labour.
    (2) Responsible manual labour.
    (3) Automatic brain workers.
    (4) Responsible brain workers.

But the matter is one perhaps for the satirist of manners
rather than the economist.   It suffices for our purpose
that the distinctions, however vague, are very real.

It is obvious the mobility of labour between the occupations of a platelayer and a barrister is not very great. It may seem perhaps to be even smaller than it is. For here it is important to bear in mind a general consideration which is equally applicable to horizontal movements within any social grade. There may be a considerable movement of labour between different employments without any individual worker having to change his occupation. The personnel of any industry is constantly changing. At one end, men die, retire, or are pensioned off; at the other end, young recruits are taken on. By a diversion of the new recruits from one employment to another, a radical change can be made in the occupational census in a comparatively short space of time. It is in this manner that such movement as takes place is largely effected at the present time. Within the ranks of the professional classes, a man does not commonly leave the profession to which he has been trained. But his *choice* of profession is determined by him or his parents not solely on pecuniary grounds but usually with an anxious scanning of the general prospects, which include pecuniary advantages together with many other things. The same thing is true in no small measure of manual wage-earners. This general consideration must be borne in mind throughout the remainder of this chapter.

But even the sons of platelayers do not commonly practise at the Bar. The obstacles in the way are various and subtle. Many of them are ideas, inherited from a bygone epoch, about keeping other people " in their proper stations," which the whole drift of circumstance, and the spirit of the age are rapidly wearing down. In the new world such obstacles are rare. But an obstacle of a more tangible and formidable kind arises from the fact that the liberal professions and many business careers require a long and expensive education and training, which the platelayer is quite unable to afford to give his son.

Now this expense of training is highly relevant not only to " what is." but to " what should be." It includes, it should be observed, a negative as well as a positive element ; a long period of waiting before income begins, as well as the actual outlay on educational and other charges. When the burden both of the waiting and the positive costs must be borne either by the individual or the family, there are few people who would seriously dispute that this goes to justify, on grounds of fairness as well as of expediency, a higher level of annual remuneration later on ; though many people would doubtless argue that the amenities and dignities of the professions should be taken into account on the other side. But the same consideration makes it a matter of legitimate doubt whether it would be desirable, even as an ideal, that the community should provide so completely the costs of training and of maintenance in the waiting period, as to make it no longer " fair " that the individual should be remunerated more highly than workers in less expensive occupations. For this would mean that more labour would be absorbed in the former employments than in principle would be socially desirable, for reasons which the argument of the next chapter will make plain. But the most desirable number of doctors, barristers, teachers, etc., is not a thing which can be settled on purely economic grounds, and it is unprofitable to carry further this particular line of thought. Few people would advocate, as an ultimate ideal, that the remuneration of the professional grades of labour should exceed that of lower grades by *more* than the extra expense of training and waiting they involve. That the excess is usually greater than this at the present time seems very probable : though it is a matter on which it is very hard to generalize. But it would certainly be far greater than it is if the principle of *laissez-faire* ruled supreme in these affairs. Fortunately it does not, and has never done so. Even before the days of free elementary education, the endowment of education was not unknown. The ancient public schools and universities, which have come down to us from the Middle Ages, are a standing witness to what in this field a far poorer community thought fit to do. Their systems of scholarships and exhibitions, no less than their courts and towers, deserve our notice. For these were designed to form what we now call " a ladder " by which talent could climb from the humblest origins to the callings which then seemed the summit either of spiritual or of worldly ambition.

This reference to " talent " makes it well to consider here a factor which necessarily complicates, though it does not substantially affect, the whole argument of the present chapter. There are differences of natural ability, which no education or training can obliterate, which it should rather be their business to excite. These differences are associated to a great extent with differences of occupation ; they *should be* so associated far more closely than in fact they are. They are also associated with differences of remuneration even within the same occupation ; "what should be" here is a question which we may excuse ourselves from discussing. The principle which, however vague, is sufficient for our present purpose is that the same *natural ability* should command the same reward in all occupations, subject to differences which should not exceed the differences of educational cost and initial waiting they involve. We cannot assert, as an economic law, that this is generally true in fact. If ever it becomes true, it will be due not to "*laissez-faire*," or "free competition," but to social arrangements, which express a sense of what is right.

§ 7. *The Apportionment of Labour among Occupations.*
When we pass to the apportionment of labour among different occupations in the same social grade, the same principle as to "what should be" applies in a simpler form. Equal natural ability should command an equal reward in all occupations ; assuming that differences in cost of training can be ignored. The reward must, of course, be interpreted not in terms of money only but of "real wages," with allowance for the varying amenities of different tasks. Now it was here that the extreme advocates of *laissez-faire* made one of their cardinal mistakes. They assumed that this ideal would be best secured by " perfect competition." The employer would choose the worker who would come for the lowest wage ; the worker would choose the employer who would pay him the highest wage ; and so, by a process similar to the higgling of a commodity market, the desirable uniform wage-level would become established.

But in fact the conditions of the labour market differ greatly from those of a commodity market. People are ignorant, do not look ahead, cannot afford to risk the loss of a job, however wretched, which they happen to have got. For reasons such as these, a considerable departure from *laissez-faire* is necessary in order to realize the theoretical results of *laissez-faire*. To prevent the putting of boys in large numbers into " blind alley " occupations, you must supplement the foresight of parents with Juvenile Employment Exchanges and After-Care Committees. To secure a proper uniformity of wages within the same occupation, you must have trade unions. To secure a proper uniformity between different occupations, you must have again trade unions, or, failing them, Trade Boards.

That the actions of trade unions are very largely of this type is a fact insufficiently appreciated by the middle-class public. The elaborate system of piece-rate lists which has been evolved in the Lancashire cotton industry is primarily designed to secure the same wage for workers of equal efficiency in all mills, irrespective of the degree to which the machinery is antiquated or up to date. This result is wholly to the good : not only does it secure " fairness " for the worker, it stimulates the employer wonderfully to efficiency. The same result could never be secured so effectively by the free play of competition. But this tendency, which is perhaps the predominant element in the trade union regulations of the cotton trade, is at least an important element in the policy of " The Common Rule " of all trade unions, though it may often be mixed up with the more questionable tendency to eliminate differences of pay for differences of natural ability, and the unquestionably bad tendency to discourage output. As between different occupations, the insistence of a trade union that wages must be levelled up towards the wages obtaining in similar trades acts again as a far more powerful force than competition.

But the actions of trade unions are by no means wholly of this type. They often serve rather to secure still higher wages for workers who, comparatively speaking, are already highly paid. It makes little difference whether this effect is secured directly by wage demands, or indirectly by restricting the right of the entry to the trade. In either case the consequences are the same, and there should be no ambiguity as to their nature. They are certainly bad for the community, certainly bad for the *other* workers of the grade, almost certainly bad for the workers of the grade regarded as a whole. The higher wages must raise the money costs of production, and result, sooner or later, in fewer workpeople being employed in that occupation ; larger numbers must accordingly seek employment elsewhere ; and this cannot but depress the wage rates of less strongly organized trades. Thus the effect is twofold : a larger proportion of workpeople will be employed in badly paid occupations ; and the wages there will be lessened.

The power of a strong trade union to secure wage advances of this type is considerable, but it must not be exaggerated. Trade unions employ as a matter of course devices which, in the case of trusts, we regard as the extremest weapons of monopoly. To say, " If you buy from anyone except us, you must not buy at a lower price than ours," which Messrs. J. & P. Coats are represented as having done, is analogous to insisting that if non-unionists are employed, it shall be at the trade union rate, as every trade union very properly insists. To say, "You must buy *only* from us," the method of the boycott, as it is called, is analogous to the very common refusal to work with non-unionists at all. But in one important respect the tactical position of a trade union is weaker than that of an ordinary combination. It has usually got a buyers' combination up against it, in the shape of an association of employers. The latter will be governed in their attitude towards the workpeople's demands, not only by immediate expediency, but also by their own sense of "what should be"; and they will usually resist demands for wages greatly in excess of those obtaining in comparable trades. In this way, the tendency for workers of the same efficiency to receive the same real wages in all employments is far stronger than might at first sight appear.

If we had to rely for this result upon trade unions alone, it would be highly problematical. For here a psychological curiosity emerges, which, familiar and intelligible as it is, is none the less a curiosity. So far from still higher wages for well-paid workpeople being regarded in the world of manual labour as detrimental to the interests of other workpeople, it has become almost a point of honour to believe the contrary. A wage dispute in a particular trade is conceived as an engagement in a far-flung battle between Capital and Labour, in which success at any part of the line will facilitate the victory of the whole army. This conception contains a measure of truth, as regards immediate and purely temporary effects; though, even here, it is made to seem unduly plausible by the recurrence of trade cycles, which cause wages at any time to move in the same direction all along the line. But, if the foregoing analysis has been appreciated, the essential falsity of this notion should be evident. It is an illusion, which should receive no endorsement, either tacit or express, in any work on economics. The general wage level of a country cannot be regarded (except temporarily, and within narrow limits) as a function of the efficiency of labour organization; it depends on the far deeper economic facts set out in §3 above.

Let us now try to summarize the conclusions of this section. There *is* a tendency towards a uniformity of real wages for workers of the same grade and of the same efficiency. This tendency is not due to competition alone. It is helped by many acts of a collective kind, arising from a sense of "what should be": it is obstructed by other acts of a like kind, where the sense of "what should be" is based on imperfect understanding. The more people act in accordance with "what should be," and the better their understanding, the more will this tendency approximate to an accurate economic law.

§ 8. *Women's Wages.* The wages of women represent a problem of great public interest, upon which the principles laid down in this chapter have a most important bearing, and which in its turn serves to illustrate these principles further. It has been suggested that male

and female labour can be regarded as a strong case of
Joint Supply, and the suggestion is not merely facetious.
The essential point, that the proportions of available
male and female labour are fairly constant (not that
they may not alter with time and circumstances, but
that they are essentially independent of the conditions
of demand) holds true not only of a country as a whole,
but hardly less of a particular district. If men and
women are to be regarded as separate grades, they are
grades between which immobility is complete. Now
men and women differ in many ways which affect both
the demand for and the supply of their services. On
the one hand, far fewer women wish to enter business
employments of any kind, as women have plenty of
work that must be done at home. On the other hand,
though women can do many kinds of work as well as
or better than men, it so happens that for much the
greater number of services, which are in large demand
in the business world, men are the more efficient.
Incidentally, it happens that many occupations which
women *might* do as well as men are closed to them by
exclusive regulations. The resultant of these forces
is that men and women are for the most part employed
in different occupations, and the scale of payment
in women's occupations is far lower than that in men's.
Of this last fact singularly small complaint is made.

It is otherwise, however, when we come to occupations
where men are either wholly or partially employed,
where women are at least approximately as efficient
as men, and where the barriers to their entry are at
least formally removed. There a ferocious controversy
rages over what is known as the principle of " equal

pay for equal work." It is easy to understand why
the male trade unionists in, let us say, the engineering
trades, should support this claim. It is also, indeed,
intelligible why the enthusiasts for Women's Rights
should urge it ; but it is much more doubtful whether
they are wise. Possibly they are wise enough in their
generation, since it might not serve them on this matter
to get across the men. But it is clearly not prudential
considerations of this kind by which they are mainly
actuated. They make the demand, with extreme
intensity of feeling, as a demand for fundamental
justice. They are also very obviously inspired with the
belief (similar to the illusion which is a point of honour
with the male trade unionist) that high wages for women
in well-paid occupations will help to raise the wages
of sweated women workers in other trades.

Now, here again, any lack of candour would be
inexcusable. The effect of this policy on the wages
in women's trades is certainly to reduce them. The
policy serves, as powerfully as any trade union custom,
to restrict the entry of women into the men's employments, and often spells virtual exclusion. For the
" equal efficiency " may be approximate only, and there
may be advantages in male labour from the employer's
standpoint which are none the less important, because
they are not easy to define. Moreover, from the
employer's standpoint, the efficacy of female labour
will be largely a matter for *experiment*, and " equal pay "
will give him no inducement to experiment at all.
The diminished number of women in these occupations
(as compared with what might have been) increases
the number who must fall back on the purely women's

trades ; and it *must* serve to reduce the wages there, where organization is by no means strong. I am far from asserting that this consideration is conclusive against the principle of " equal pay for equal work " (though I think it conclusive against a rigid interpretation of it) ; for other matters, such as the standpoint of the male trade unionist must be taken into account. But the reactions on the wages in women's trades permit of no ambiguity.

In occupations of another type, the issue takes a somewhat different form. In the teaching profession, " equal pay " would not exclude the women ; it would be far more likely to exclude the men. For, though the advocates of the principle would declare that their intention is that the salaries of women should be levelled up to those of men, it is more probable that the ultimate outcome would be a levelling down. Educational authorities have the ratepayer and the taxpayer to consider ; and, apart from this, they have their own interpretation of " what should be." To pay a woman less than a man for the same work may seem glaringly unfair ; but it is not very clear why a woman, who is an elementary school teacher, should be paid much more than, say, a hospital nurse, merely because in the former case a number of men happen also to be employed. In fact, there is a clashing of equities in this connection ; and there is little doubt which of them the educational authorities would prefer. A levelling down of the men's salaries would make it all but impossible to attract men of the desired type into the profession, and would thus lead to the virtual extinction of the male elementary school teacher. This might

seem in a narrow sense to be economically desirable.
Why should not men take their services to the tasks
for which they can command a higher reward, and which
women cannot do as well? But whether this would
be desirable in the true interests of education is a far
more doubtful matter. And this is the real problem
of "equal pay for equal work" for male and female
school teachers. The reader will notice that I
have refrained from alluding to the controversy
as to whether men should receive more on the
grounds that they have wives and families to
maintain. That, although a most absorbing issue,
is not the real issue in practice at the present time.
The real issue is a clashing between a sense of "what
should be" on obvious general grounds and a sense
of "what should be" in the particular, derived from
the very patent and general "what is" that men
receive as a rule far higher pay than women.

CHAPTER X

THE REAL COSTS OF PRODUCTION

§ 1. *Comparative Costs.* Beneath the great diversity of the considerations which are applicable to the different agents of production, certain general conclusions emerge from the analysis of the last four chapters. In no case did we find that the aggregate supply of the agent was determined by clear and certain economic laws, possessing any fundamental significance. The supply of natural resources is a fixed thing, quite independent of the efforts or the desires of man. However the supply of capital and the supply of labour may react under present conditions towards economic stimuli, these reactions possess no quality of inevitability and bear no clear relation to " what should be." The supply of risk-bearing responds perhaps more decidedly to the prospects of increased reward ; but it is so intimately associated with special knowledge and the qualities of business enterprise, as to leave some uncertainty attaching even to this conclusion. When, on the other hand, we turn to the apportionment of these factors among different uses, we find relations which are both clear and fundamental. Laws emerge which state at once not only " what is " or at least " what tends to be," but also " what should

162

be " ; and it is the fact that they state " what should be " that gives them their fundamental character.

These conclusions enable us to give a general answer to the question which was raised at the end of Chapter V : What are the ultimate real costs to which the money cost of production corresponds ? The attempt has often been made to relate money costs to such things as the effort of working and the sacrifice of waiting. The existence of such costs is beyond dispute. Much saving does mean a sacrifice of immediate enjoyment to the man who saves. Most labour is irksome and disagreeable in itself, and involves strain and wear and tear ; while all labour means a deprivation of the utility of leisure. Workpeople, moreover, do not grow on gooseberry bushes, but must be fed and clothed from the cradle ; and their rearing and maintenance represents a real cost which someone must incur.

But the existence (or the importance) of such costs is one thing, their relation to money costs is another. In Chapter VIII we saw how difficult it was to establish any clear relation between the rate of interest and the sacrifice of saving. The costs of labour present similar difficulties. The relative irksomeness of two occupations may affect the relative wages which will rule in the two cases ; so, certainly, will the differences in the cost of education and training which they require. But these are matters which concern the *apportionment* of labour between different employments. There is no good reason to suppose that the general wage-level would be reduced, merely because work as a whole became less irksome, or involved a smaller physical or mental strain. The supply of people is not determined

M

by the same kind of influences as is the supply of
a commodity.   Parents do not produce children for
the sake of the wages which the children will receive
when they go out to work ; or, if this happens, we rightly
regard it as a horrible anomaly.   In so far as parents
are affected by economic conditions it is by their own
economic conditions ; the question is rather one of
how many children they can afford to have, than of a
balancing of the cost to them against the incomes
which their children may subsequently acquire.   But
other considerations enter in ; and, in fact, it is doubtful
how the aggregate supply of labour will react to changes
in prosperity.   Finally, the supply of land involves
neither effort nor sacrifice ; and, among our money
costs, we have to account for the item of the rent of land.
To dispose of this difficulty by arguing that rent does
not enter into marginal costs (in any sense which is not
equally true of wages and profits) is to lose contact
with reality.   Thus the attempt to explain money
costs in terms of the costs of producing the ultimate
agents of production leads us into a quagmire of unreality
and dubious hypothesis.   For a systematic theory, which
will rest on firm foundations, we must interpret money
costs in very different terms.

The real costs which the price of a commodity
measures are not absolute, but comparative.   Marginal
money costs reduce themselves in the last analysis
to the payments which must be made to secure the use
of the requisite agents of production.   These payments
tend to equal the payments which the same agents
could have commanded in alternative employments.
The payments which they could have commanded in

alternative employments, tend in their turn to equal
the derived marginal utilities of their services in those
employments.   It is thus the loss of *Utility* which
arises from the fact that these agents of production
are not available for alternative employments that is
measured by the money costs of a commodity at the
margin of production.

This conception of ultimate costs encounters an
instinctive repugnance, arising from a mistaken sense
of logical symmetry, which it will be well to examine.
Cost, it is objected, so interpreted loses its character
as an independent entity.   It is merely something
derived from utility.   Now in the earlier chapters
of this volume, we found reason to be impressed with
the general symmetry which pervades the relations
of demand and supply.   Moreover, when we considered
the case of ordinary commodities we found that at
the back of demand and giving rise to it was utility ;
at the back of supply, and limiting it, was cost.   The
general symmetry between demand and supply thus
seemed almost to imply a fundamental symmetry
between utility and cost.   If, then, cost in the last
analysis is derived from utility, does not this make
nonsense of the symmetry between demand and supply,
or, if we cling to this last symmetry as a demonstrable
truth, must we not refuse to admit that cost can be
derived from utility ?

This is one of those false dilemmas which supply the
wiseacres of the world with a plausible case for dis-
trusting the logical faculty.   If we have good reason for
believing that both of two apparently inconsistent
things are true, the explanation is seldom that one of

them is really false ; it is more usually that they are not really inconsistent. So it is here. The symmetry between demand and supply is very great, and we should always look to see if it holds good, but it is by no means perfect, and it is in the last analysis that it most notably fails. It is most important to distinguish clearly between the utility and the cost of a commodity as two separate and independent things. In Chapter V, it will be remembered, we did not permit ourselves to derive the costs of producing cotton lint from the utility of cotton-seed. The refusal to do so was essential to clear thought ; it led to some very useful practical corollaries. But to derive the cost of a commodity from the utility of something which is produced *with* it, as part of the same productive process ; and to derive the cost from the utilities which the agents, which help to produce it, possess for other purposes, are two entirely different things. In works on International Trade, the reader will discover that the comparative nature of real costs is so unmistakable that a Doctrine of Comparative Costs is expounded with much formality at the outset. This doctrine is apt to prove somewhat puzzling, when we have to deal with it as an apparent exception to the general tenor of economic theory. Its difficulties disappear when we realize clearly that the real cost of *anything* is the curtailment of the supply of other useful things, which the production of that particular thing entails.

§ 2. *The Allocation of Resources.* However strange the above conception may seem, there should be no doubt that this cost is very " real." Here the irregularities and maladjustments of the economic world, the recurrence of trade depressions and the like, do much to obscure a clear vision of the essential realities. At a time when there is much unemployment, and much machinery standing idle, it is so clear to common sense that we *could* produce more of some particular thing without diminishing the supply of other things, that any apparent statement to the contrary may perhaps seem the height of academic pedantry. But let me ask the reader to consider with an open mind a familiar parallel. During the recent war there was inevitably much waste and muddle in the utilization of the military resources of the Allies. Some regiments would be kept inactive for long periods, not for purposes of rest or training, but owing to some defect of organization. In the manufacture of munitions, an insufficient appreciation of the principles of joint demand led to the piling up of excessive stores of certain materials, which were useless until commensurate supplies of the complementary factors could be obtained. It is unnecessary to multiply examples. The waste of both man-power and material was immense. But the allocation of these resources between, for instance, the various theatres of war was none the less a very real problem, which gave rise to much engrossing controversy. It was an axiom that the more resources you employed in Mesopotamia or in Palestine, the less resources remained available for France. No one thought of maintaining that, as long as there was any waste of these resources, so long as there remained any men to be "combed out" of unessential industries, you could pour troops and munitions into Salonika without stopping to consider

the needs of other theatres of war. Such a notion would
have been clearly imbecile, for the sufficient reason
that the sending of armies to Salonika would do nothing
in itself to secure (however much it might incidentally
stimulate) the more efficient use of the resources which
remained.

Now this is precisely analogous to the problem of
the allocation of our resources for the purposes of peace.
Notwithstanding all the wastes and maladjustments
of the economic system, the use of resources to produce
one commodity *does* in general curtail the production
of others. The mere launching of a new business enterprise does no more than the sending of an army to
Salonika, to eliminate waste in the remainder of the
economic organism. Unemployment, broadly speaking,
is a function not of the magnitude of the normal demand
for labour (which affects rather the wage-level), but of
fluctuations in the demand for labour ; fluctuations
from one day to another as at the docks, from one
season to another as in the building trades, above all
from one period of years to another as in the cycles of
general trade boom and depression. Nothing will
diminish unemployment which does not serve to
diminish these fluctuations. A new business will not,
as a rule, have any such effect. If it is launched
during a trade depression (a most unusual proceeding),
it may temporarily absorb unemployed labour and idle
materials. But when the next boom comes, it will
be using, though presumably to greater advantage,
labour and materials which, but for it, would have
been employed for other purposes. Meanwhile the
causes making for unemployment will be unaffected.

Miscalculations will still be made, the building trades will still become slack in the winter, the casual methods of engaging dock labourers will still continue, trade cycles will still recur, while beneath them, and concealed by them, some industries will expand and others will decay. Thus, like the armies at Salonika, the new business would in effect divert resources from elsewhere.

This truth needs to be firmly grasped in mind. It is this that makes it in general unsound policy to subsidize industries, either directly or indirectly, by means of a protective tariff. It is this, indeed, that supplies the answer to half the economic fallacies that are always current.

The allocation of resources so as to yield the maximum effect was rightly recognized as one of the most vital and difficult of our war-time problems. To cope with it, the Allied peoples devised one instrument after another, and finally evolved the Supreme Allied Council. The analagous problem in the economic world of peace time is no less important and far more difficult; but there is nothing to correspond to The Supreme Allied Council. There we rely upon a co-operation which, as was stressed in Chapter I, is unco-ordinated. That co-operation has been evolved by the mutual competition of innumerable business concerns, controlled by men largely animated by the motive of pecuniary profit. But it has not been evolved wholly by such means: and how far that competition or that motive of profit is essential to its efficiency are questions with which this volume has not been in any way concerned. The economic laws, the relations between utility, and price and cost, with which it has been occupied, are an entirely different matter ; and these *are* essential to the efficiency of any system of society. For if the marginal utility of a commodity is equal to its marginal cost, and if this marginal cost is composed of payments to the various agents of production at least as great as they could have obtained if they had been used otherwise, this amounts to saying that the agents of production are so utilized as to yield the maximum utility ; and this is the same thing as saying that they are so utilized as to produce the maximum wealth.

§ 3. *Utility and Wealth.* Upon this last point it is important to be quite clear. An increase in wealth seems a solid, tangible reality ; something, which, however much we may scorn it in our more precious moods, we recognize, for a rather poor community, to be an important object of endeavour. But an increase in utility seems a vague, impalpable notion, hardly deserving the same practical concern. None the less the two things are identical. We greatly deceive ourselves if we suppose wealth to be an objective reality. It is true that, when we get behind the money in which it is measured, we come upon commodities, like food and clothes and houses and factories, which seem comfortably solid and objective things ; but we also come upon many services, like those of gardeners and doctors and hospital nurses, which we are bound to reckon as part of our wealth, although they are not embodied in any tangible commodities. Moreover, although material commodities are objective realities in themselves, and in many of their properties, they are *not* objective realities in their property as wealth. A pair of boots is an objective fact ; so is the number of pairs in existence at any time, so is their size, their weight, the quantity of leather or of paper which they happen to contain. But the wealth which those boots represent is not an objective fact. It depends upon the opinion which men and women entertain as to their utility ; and these opinions take us into the subjective regions of human psychology. Let us suppose, for instance, that we calculated, on the basis of present prices, that the boots in existence at the present time represented $\frac{1}{1000}$ part of our total wealth. Suppose, then, that a miracle were to happen ; that the skies opened and rained boots upon us, of every size and shape and pattern, until we had 1000 times as many boots as we had before. Could we say that our total real wealth had been doubled ? Clearly we could not. To obtain boots for nothing, and to wear a new pair every week, would make us somewhat better off, but not twice as well off as we were previously. In other words, the real wealth of a thousand times as many boots as we have now, is not a thousand times as great as the wealth of the present number of boots. We are, indeed, practically restating the Law of Diminishing Utility ; and this perhaps is enough to show that wealth is fundamentally the same thing as utility.

Another point, however, is worth noting. Our real wealth would be somewhat increased in the case supposed ; but if we were to turn to the money measure of wealth, the opposite result would be far more likely. For the price of boots would most likely fall to nothing, and the total value of boots, in the commercial sense, would accordingly be nothing also. This shows that money values may be a most imperfect measure of aggregate wealth ; for what money values represent is the product of the quantity of the commodity and its *marginal* utility, while aggregate wealth is *total* utility, which is a very different thing. This, it may be observed, makes all attempts to compare the wealth of different countries or different times, and no less to construct Index Numbers of Prices, imperfect of necessity, and arbitrary in their foundations.

§ 4. *Criteria of Policy.* The point has now been reached at which we must take into account the very important fact which was mentioned at the close of Chapter III. The maximum utility which the laws of supply and demand tend to bring about is a maximum *total* utility indeed, but one still measured in terms of money. An unequal distribution of wealth destroys any necessary correspondence between that and the maximum *real* utility. This consideration, however, does not affect the general validity of the conclusion that the laws of supply and demand represent what is socially desirable now or under any system. For what is at fault here is the distribution of wealth ; and it is that which should be changed, in so far as it is possible to do so. Now it is important to realize that whenever it is possible to supply a commodity to poor people below cost price, it is possible to alter the distribution of wealth, for that in effect is what is done. Purchasing power, which may be taken from richer people by taxation, or which may be obtained from " collective " profits on other trading, is in effect transferred to the poor people in question, though the transference is coupled with the condition that the purchasing power must be expended in a particular way. It is *in general* desirable that the transference should be made without this condition being attached. To this general statement, exceptions indeed exist so numerous and important as possibly to justify a great extension of social expenditure of this type. Education should certainly be provided free of charge, there are strong arguments for subsidizing housing; the provision of milk to expectant mothers, the feeding of school children, such instances can be multiplied into a very extensive list. But it is important to observe that in each case the justification of the policy rests in the presumption that the service supplied is one which it is particularly important that the beneficiaries should have, *as compared with* the other things upon which they might have preferred to expend the equivalent purchasing power, had it been transferred to them without conditions. Where there is no such presumption, as surely there is none in the case of the great bulk of commodities, the relation between price and marginal cost should be rigidly maintained; it is the distribution of purchasing power which we should rather seek to alter. How far is it possible to alter that ?

I suppose that it is inevitable that many readers will have concluded that the preceding chapters must be taken to mean that the distribution of wealth is not susceptible of any appreciable change. I would remind those readers of an important distinction upon which impatient people have sometimes based a complaint against economists. The economist, it is said, analyses with great pomp and ceremony the laws governing the distribution of wealth among the agents of production, but says practically nothing about the distribution between individuals and classes, which is the only thing of any real interest to practical people. Now the economist concentrates on the agents of production for the very good reason that it is only with respect to them that any clear and certain laws as to distribution can be laid down. Into the distribution between individuals and classes there enter other and variable factors, governed by no fundamental economic law; and *here*, the conclusion should at once suggest itself, is the field for action designed to alter the distribution of wealth. What is possible or desirable in this field, it is again not the purpose of this volume to discuss. It is an obvious, even if not a very helpful conclusion that an increase in the habit of saving among weekly wage-earners might, without appreciably affecting the distribution between Capital and Labour, greatly modify the resulting distribution between social classes. But questions as to how far it might be possible or justifiable to achieve a similar result by the use of the weapon of taxation, by changes in inheritance laws, or by the public ownership of industry take us into a far more uncertain and controversial sphere. The difficulties and objections which present themselves are familiar and formidable; but they are of quite a different order from the economic laws which we have been examining. The laws themselves do not entitle us to make any dogmatic pronouncement upon these large issues of social policy.

But this is not to deprive these laws of practical importance. They represent essential criteria of sound policy in the sphere of social reorganization no less than in ordinary business. In our days a curious obsession has led many people to disparage these criteria, as though they were the sordid prejudices of a stupid tradesman. Because it has been found a matter of obvious practical convenience to maintain the roads out of taxation or of rates, and to dispense with charges for their use, it is suggested that the same principle should be applied to the railways. Or, more commonly, because it has been found convenient to make the same charge for the carrying of letters between Land's End and John o' Groats as between Hampstead and Highgate, it is suggested that *this* principle should be applied to railway rates and fares. It may be well, therefore, to point out that the justification of uniform postal charges rests upon the facts : (1) that the costs of collection, sorting, etc., are so large a part of the costs of carrying a letter, that the real cost between John o' Groats and Land's End does not differ from that between Hampstead and Highgate by as much as might at first sight appear, (2) that the charges in any case are very small ; so that (3) the avoidance of the small degree of taxes and bounties which the present system implies is not worth the book-keeping expenses which differential charges would involve. It should be obvious that these considerations apply to the railways with a greatly diminished force. They might possibly justify what is known as the " zone " system of charges, i.e. uniform rates within certain narrow areas. But the notion of uniform rates throughout Great Britain conjures up a vision of trains taking coal from South Wales to Scotland, and others taking coal from Scotland

to South Wales, in accordance with the slightest prefer-
ences of the consumers, and without regard to the
extra real cost involved, on a scale to which the " wastes
of competition " afford no parallel. It would in fact
achieve the essential folly of " sending coals to New-
castle." These considerations, however, are not what
interest the advocates of the postal principle. They
seem to recommend the obliteration or the confusion of
the relations between price and cost as a superior ideal.
It is important to be clear what exactly this ideal
involves.

It involves, in the first place, as the whole argument
of this volume has gone to show, a less economical
employment of our productive resources; they would
be diverted to ends of less utility, and so produce less
real wealth. But this is not the worst. There is plenty
of waste and maladjustment in our economic system at
the present time. The desirable relation of price to
marginal cost is but imperfectly attained. The further
departures from this relation, which would follow from
any likely applications of the postal principle, might not
matter in themselves so very much. What is far more
serious is that the criteria of efficiency would become
blunted, and the clear aims of management would be
confused in fog. It is essential that every manager
should be on the alert to eliminate waste and to improve
efficiency, that he should be always trying to secure
the best results; but how can he do this if he has no
simple means of *measuring* what results are good and
what are bad ? The measure which he has at present
is that of price, cost and the resultant profit, and it
would be fatal to take that away, unless an equally

simple and more accurate measure could be substituted for it.

This is not a question, it should be observed, of motive or incentive. Very likely we much exaggerate the importance of the profit motive. It may be true that men would work, perhaps that they already work in fact, as zealously for a fixed salary, as for personal gain. But aim and motive are two somewhat different things, and the *aim* of profit is, and will remain, essential to the efficient conduct of business. In a game the players are not animated by the motive of scoring runs or points, but they aim at them; and the zest disappears very speedily from the game, if that aim ceases to be of interest. Moreover, while a scoring system is always a somewhat arbitrary thing, measuring imperfectly the true merits of the play, if it measures them with the roughest accuracy, we prefer the issue of our games to be decided so, rather than by the decisions of an impartial judge, who can take into account the finest points of skill. So it is in the world of business. The scoring-board of profits may be an imperfect one; let us, by all means, where we can, alter the rules of the game so as to make it better. But let us not imagine that it displays a finer insight or a superior intellect to speak as though the scoring board could be dispensed with, and the test of profit and loss treated as irrelevant. Quantitative measurement is essential to efficiency. Let us be careful to remember all that this implies.

23

PRINTED IN GREAT BRITAIN BY
WILLIAM CLOWES AND SONS, LIMITED, LONDON AND BECCLES.

85